A book

about art & design research
about making & iteration
about action & reflection
about raising questions
about points of departure
about positioning
about a process
about articulating what you do
about the circle of
      doing research

This is a book about doing research. The emphasis is on the doing as much as it is on the research.

Practice and making play an important role in art and design research. Yet there are few resources to guide you in undertaking such practice-based research. This book aims to be a guide for anyone embarking on a research project in art or design – whether beginner or advanced, student or practising professional. It offers a model that is accessible, activating and, we hope, a little demystifying of what it means to do research. It is also intended as a pedagogical tool to foster a research attitude.

In the model presented here, making is as important an action as studying sources or working with participants, and making public is seen as equally relevant to the research process as documenting and reflecting.

The following six actions make up the circle model and the six chapters of this book: research by making, research of context, participatory research, reflecting on research, documenting research and making public.

The three actions at the 'base' of the model are where information, prototypes, encounters and experiences are gathered and produced. The three actions of reflecting, documenting and publishing form the 'spinner' that turns these actions and their results into research.

At the centre of the circle is the person who makes the spinner turn – you. Moving through the different actions in a deliberate way is what makes your project a research project. Be explicit in your decisions and choices, put into words what you did and why – including what you did by intuition or what happened by chance – and support all this with documentation, images and reflections.

Where you want to start (and end) is up to you.

The circle model is an open and non-linear model. Any action can be an entry point, whether you want to start with material experiments, in the library or having conversations with others. All actions are interconnected and inform each other, encouraging a process of iteration and constant reflection. Feel free to use the book in the same way, starting wherever you feel drawn and not anticipating where it might end.

The open and accessible nature of the model – reflected in its design – is also intended to be inclusive of different skills, talents and needs. Every research project is different, and we hope that every researcher embarking on a process of inquiry will find their own way.

We describe research as an *articulated inquiry into questions and interests*. This implies an experimental and iterative process with an uncertain outcome, which is as much about experience and learning as it is about the production of knowledge.

Research in art and design has a value of its own that makes room for the unexpected and the intangible, for not-knowing, for radical questioning and for a persistence in sharing with the public. Such values require a way of working that doesn't derive from, let alone subordinate itself to, traditional or academic forms of research. We hope that this model and this book will contribute to the ongoing conversation about other forms of research and the knowledge and value they produce.

Various editorial elements are used throughout the book.

Alongside explanatory texts on each of the actions and themes, the editorial elements aim to give a sense of the breadth, depth, possibilities and surprises of art and design research. Images of art student projects show the practice of research across many different disciplines. You will find lists of examples of media, genres, audiences etc – these are far from exhaustive and you are welcome to add to them. Enumerations tell you what you need to know about the why and what of, for example, involving other people or asking a good research question. Questions in italics stimulate reflection on your own research project and process.

Exercises are included to get you started, whether it is working with sources, exploring your network or designing an interaction. Each chapter begins with a question that encourages you to think about the implications of that action within a research project, and ends with a note-taking space where you are invited to give your own answers or formulate different questions altogether. And throughout the book you will find research trajectories of art and design students that illustrate the rich possibilities in the unfolding of a research project.

The table of contents depicts the model. By opening out the cover of the book, the model can be kept next to the pages. We recommend using the table of contents as an orientation point while reading.

The circle model can be enriched with methods, sources and specific questions according to your discipline and needs. We encourage you to make it your own!

Harma Staal, Miriam Rasch, Jojanneke Gijsen

Willem de Kooning Academy (WdKA) Rotterdam, The Netherlands

When does making become research?

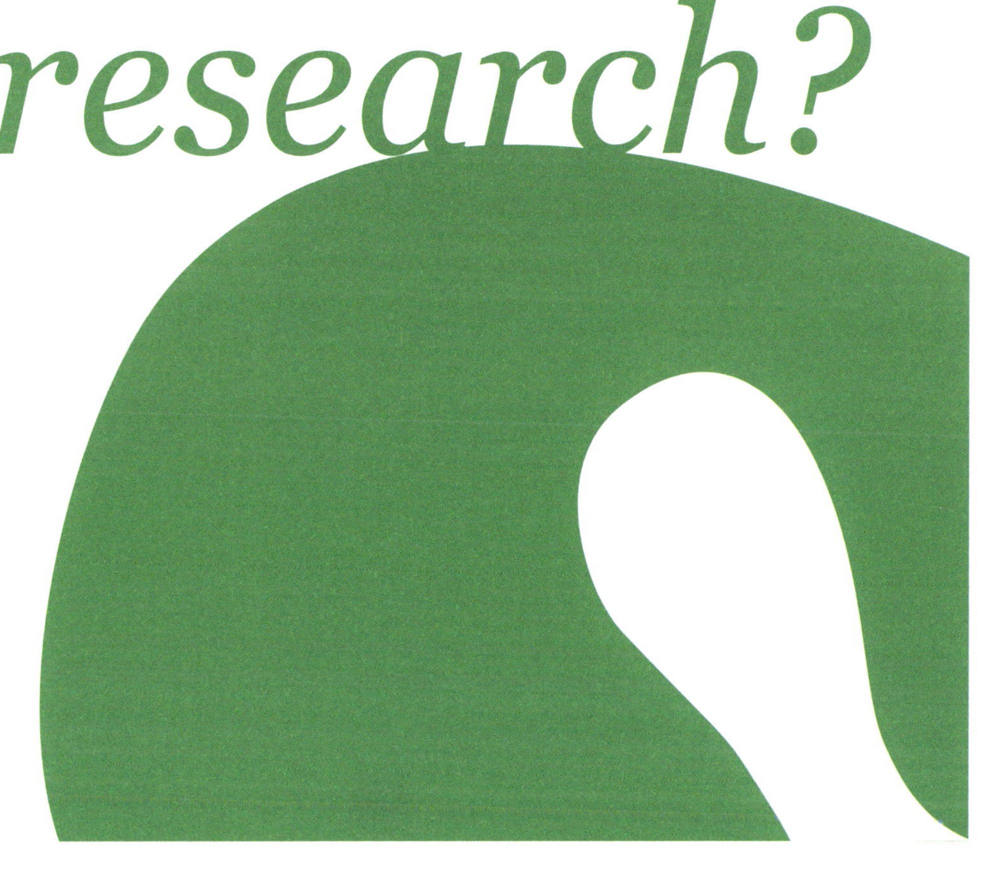

Research by making is at the heart of art and design research. It is characterised by activities such as experimentation and prototyping. It involves iteration and constant reflection on what you are doing, observing and deciding. Making isn't limited to the production of material artefacts, but can also refer to temporal and ephemeral forms, to language and writing, and to social and embodied practice. It can be individual or collaborative. Making becomes research when it is part of an articulated and shared process.

AI-generated visuals
bio-design
book binding
ceramics
choreography
composition
cooking
dance
embodied art
fashion
food design
gardening
improvisation
light design
material production
musical score
painting
performance
poetry
product design
reading
sculpture
serious games
spoken word
sound piece
theatre play
walking
workshop

There is a misconception that doing research begins with reading a lot of theory. It can just as easily begin with an act of making – taking a hundred photographs, exploring all the possibilities and constraints of a certain material, or improvising movements in a choreography.

Doing research in an artistic or design context means that your questions and actions are in some way linked to practice. Whether you are exploring a social issue, seeking a design solution or developing an educational format, it is extremely helpful to incorporate research by making from the outset. After all, making is often both the origin and the outcome of these questions and actions.

The activity of making activates the implicit or tacit knowledge of the hands and body – something that cannot be read in a book or learned from an expert. It is an embodied way of doing research that invites you to step out of your head and into the world.

Even if you are just in the studio or workshop, research by making means bringing something into the world that makes a difference. It can be an object, however undefined or messy, an interaction or an attempt to capture the intangible. It will begin to move, establish relationships and talk back to you.

For your making practice to play its part in your research, you should always document what you do. Ask lots of questions and repeat your actions over and over again.

Making as research allows you to:
> *make your research tangible from the onset;*
> *link your research to your making practice;*
> *bring depth to your practice and give theory a practical edge;*
> *tap into knowledge not found in the library;*
> *help others to relate to an issue differently;*
> *gain insight into the (im)possibilities of a given form, its aesthetics and affects.*

Making strategies help you get started in a concrete and productive way. They allow your practice to be part of your research and vice versa. In the early stages of making, what you are doing may not feel like research. It is through reflection, documentation and articulation that making can become research. What steps did you take and why? What happened and what did you learn? Use 'the riddle' (pp. 60-61) as a tool to turn your actions into research. Making strategies intertwine and are often combined.

> Making for the sake of making is all about getting into a productive flow where your intuition rules. You can use age-old methods such as automatic drawing or improvisation, or you can start from a writing prompt. Concentrate on the direction your hand is taking you. Get out of your head and into action.

> Making as a skill is about mastering materials and techniques. In the process of learning and developing your craft, unexpected results sometimes occur. These results can lead you down new paths in your research.

> Making to understand is about observing with all your senses and using technology to capture what you see, hear or feel. We perceive only a small part of the world around us. Using a pencil, camera, sound recorder or even computer vision, you can discover and make visible the invisible.

> Making as experimentation is about testing and prototyping, in order to, for example, discover new uses for a tool or material. What happens when you use a hammer as a paintbrush? What are the consequences of changing the scene of your performance piece? Try as many options as you can. Failure is part of the process, so don't be afraid to get stuck.

> Making through dialogue is a form of making where exchange and conversation with others is an integral part of the making process or end result. A designed artefact or situation can be informed by the experiences and stories of others, or it can be an invitation in and of itself to share such experiences and stories.

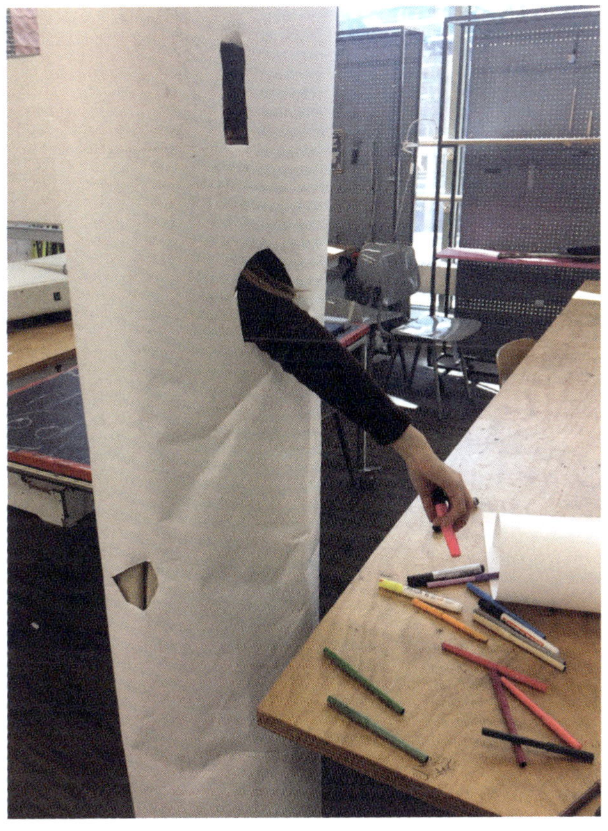

Sarah van der Pols | *Tube Drawing* | 2022 | Graduation research, BA Fine Art & Design in Education, WdKA | A research into the spatialisation of the drawing surface.

> **Unmaking** asks the uncomfortable and critical question of whether we should still be making new things in a world already flooded with stuff. How do you create without perpetuating an extractive and unsustainable system? Can you make something new out of what already exists? Unmaking looks at strategies such as hacking, upcycling and repair. Start with a trip to the second-hand shop or by taking apart a discarded machine.

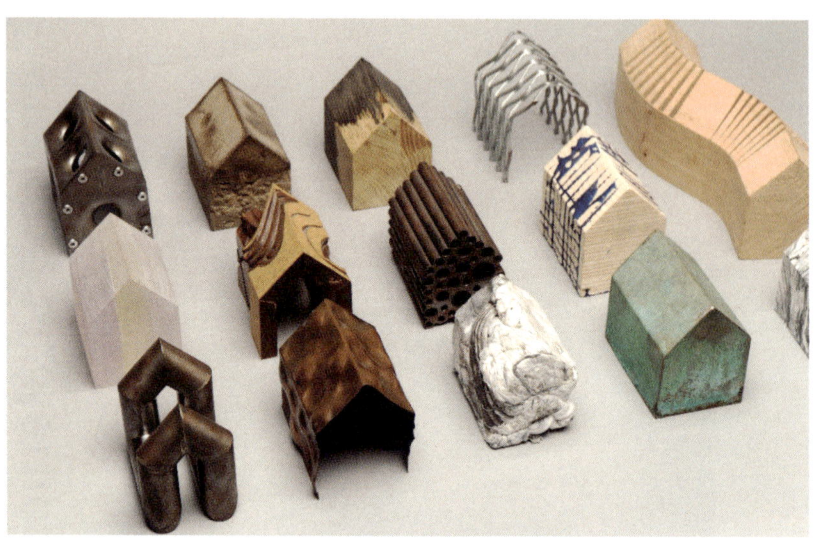

Material Station | *A Library of Materials* | Using the basic form of the house, the Material Station at WdKA carried out material research in order to get to know different materials by working with them. What are the affordances of each material and what meaning does it provoke? Each house can be seen as a small experiment or prototype.

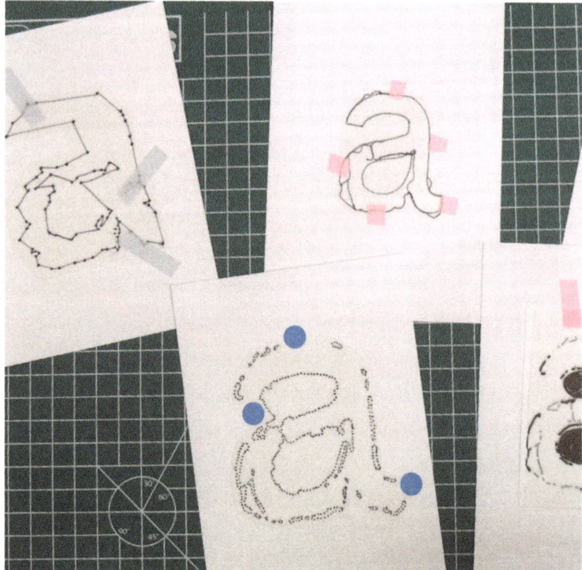

Puck van Pelt | *Typeface* | 2022 | Graduation research, BA Graphic Design, WdKA | The typeface as a starting point for material research. Deconstructing and damaging a typeface led to a new typeface design.

Material research teaches
you about the affordances
of a particular material.
What it can and cannot do, its
possibilities and limitations. Use an
iterative process to go deeper into
experimenting with any material,
whether fabric, metal, bacteria or
software, or for example by using
language as an artistic medium
or creating temporal, social or
pedagogical practices. The process
of making is about engaging in
experimentation and daring to fail.
Making prototypes throughout the
process helps you to share and
reflect on your research.

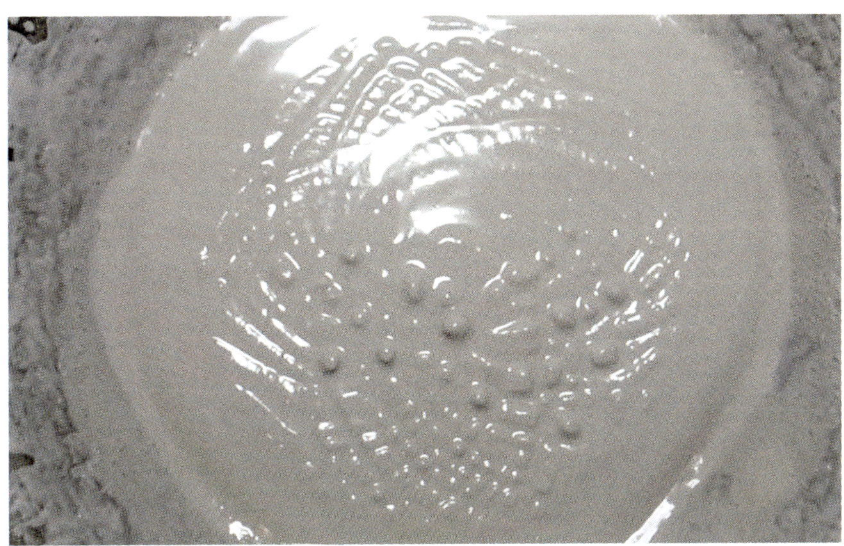

Catherine van Bijnen | *Fluid Frequency* | 2022 |
Graduation research, BA Transformation Design, WdKA |
A research in how to make the intangible tangible. Starting from
the question of what determines form, Catherine developed a
technique to shape plaster using sound frequencies. How does
sound determine the shape of the material, without any further
influence?

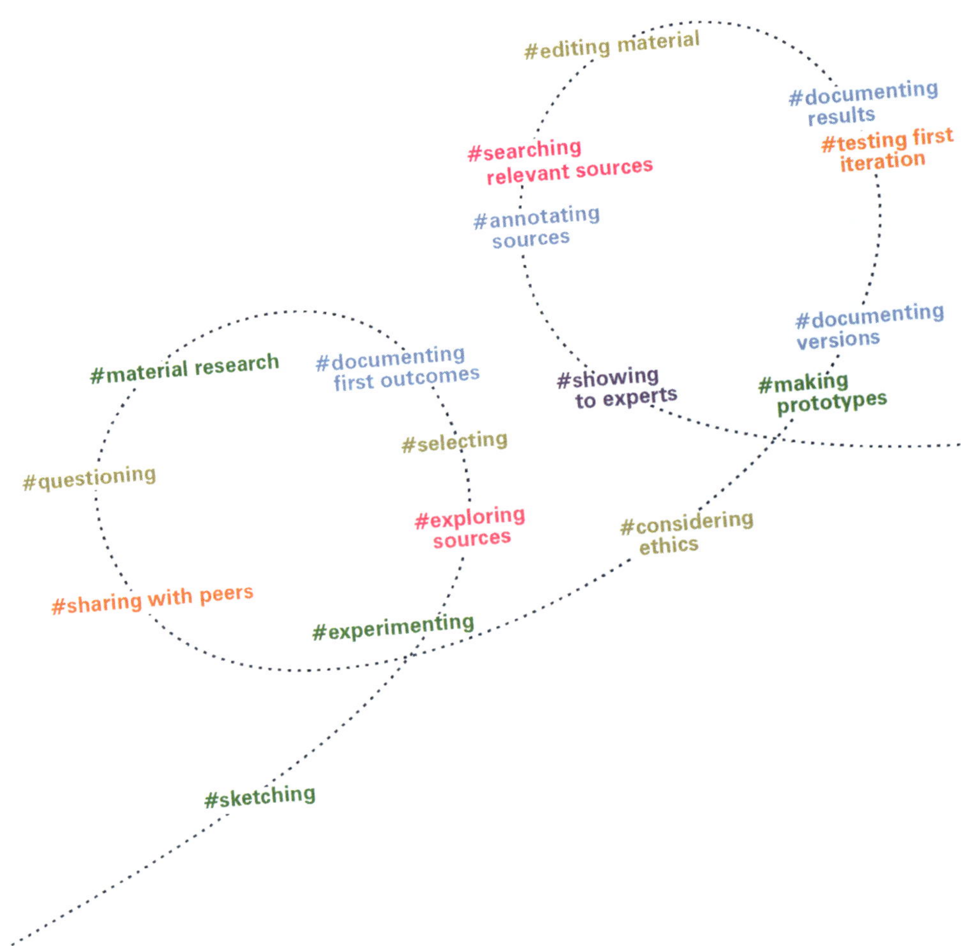
#editing material
#documenting results
#searching relevant sources
#testing first iteration
#annotating sources
#documenting versions
#material research
#documenting first outcomes
#showing to experts
#making prototypes
#selecting
#questioning
#exploring sources
#considering ethics
#sharing with peers
#experimenting
#sketching

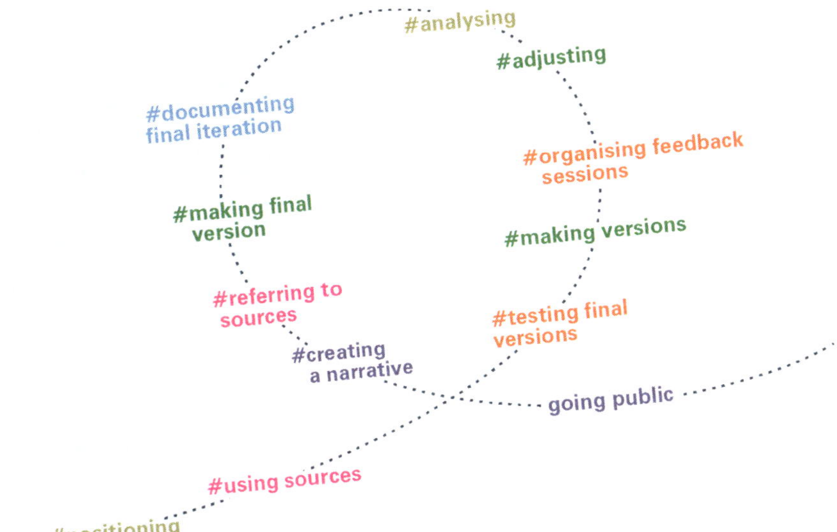

Research in art and design is characterised by iteration.

This means that you repeat certain actions over the course of your research project. Each new cycle of actions is based on the findings of the previous one. Your questions, knowledge and practice move forward by looking back and responding to what has happened. Iteration also applies to the questions you ask.

The iterative step can simply involve testing a first prototype and reflecting on the results, then moving to a new version of the prototype that can be tested again. Or it can be more extensive, like designing a process that involves different collaborators, response groups or public moments.

Look back at your process. What steps have you taken, perhaps unconsciously, and what have your actions brought about?

What differences, advances or setbacks have you encountered?

What questions do you have and what choices do you need to make?

Looking forward, where are you going next?

Iteration is particularly important in research by making. By tweaking, augmenting and repeating what you do, you can find out what still needs work or what needs rethinking. Applying what you've learned from one cycle to the next will help you refine your questions and show you where dead ends lie. The cyclical movement provides a structure for reflection and deliberation. This is where search becomes re-search.

+ Articulating what the hands and body know or intuit, or what the material wants or prohibits.

+ Documenting everything from beginning to end.

+ Going back to reflect on what has happened to decide how to move forward.

When does making become research?

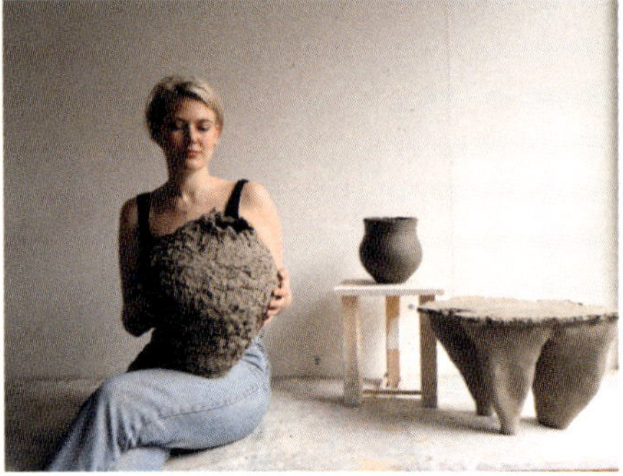

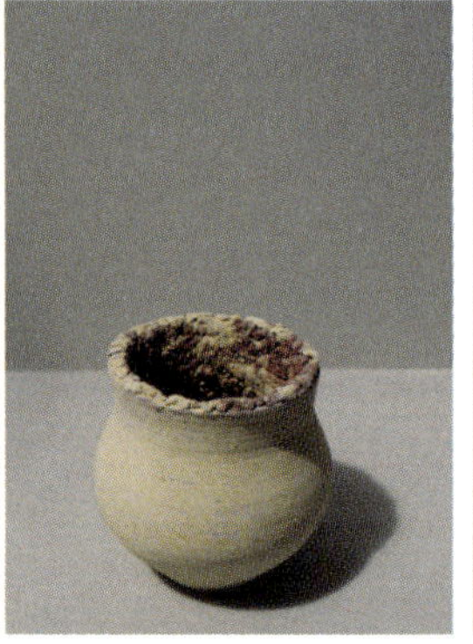

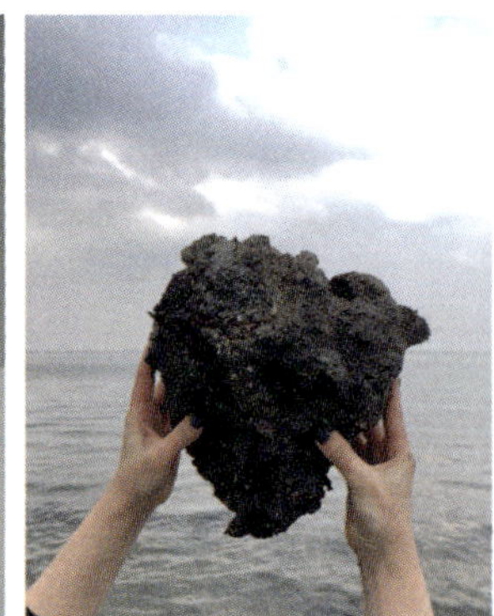

Rink Schelling | *The Muddy Collection* | 2022 | Graduation research BA, Product Design, WdKA

Rink Schelling graduated as a product designer in 2022. Her love of ceramics and of growing up in the province of Zeeland led her to research unfiltered clay from the region and whether it could be worked.

Rink not only wanted to work with clay, but also to create a book that would make her research accessible and enjoyable for everyone. To this end, she photographed and documented the process from the very start.

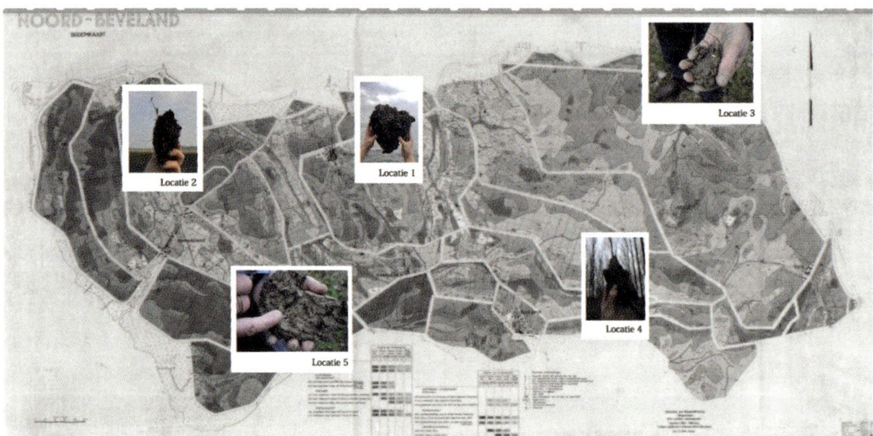

After researching sources, Rink used a geological map to narrow down her search for natural clay to a small part of Zeeland.

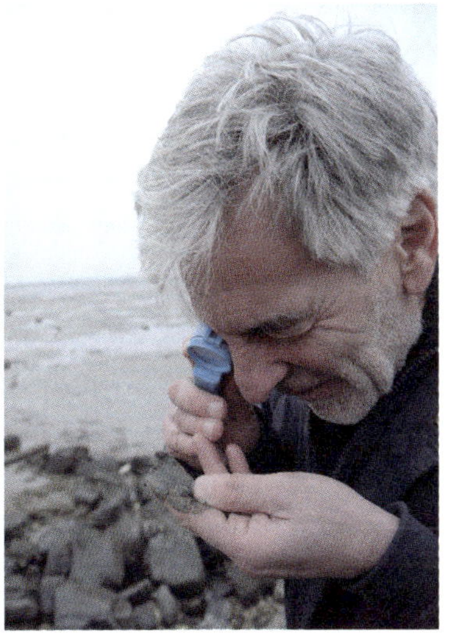

She went on a field trip with a geologist and discovered the beauty of mud, or unfiltered clay.

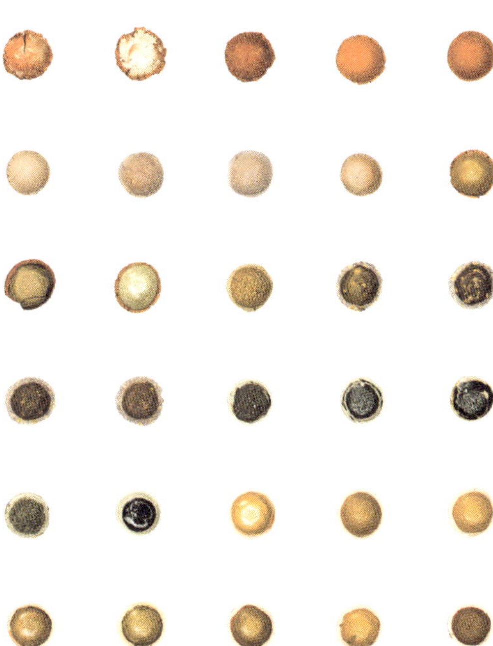

To compare and map the material, Rink decided to model all the material samples in the same format. In this way, she also compared the unfiltered with the filtered clay.

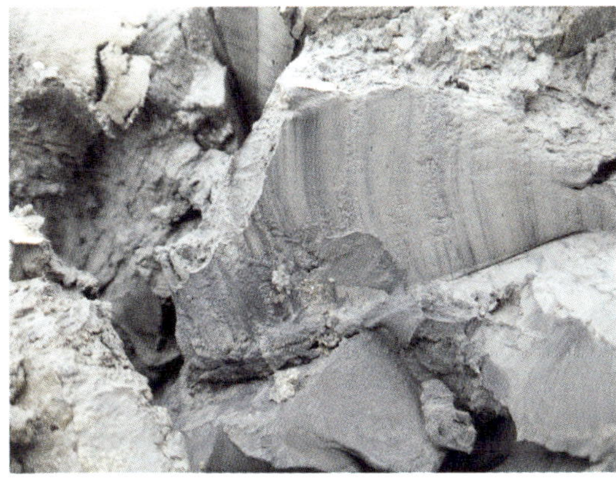

What the concept of her graduation project should be became obvious to Rink when she saw the surprising colours and patterns of the unfiltered clay through her material proofs.

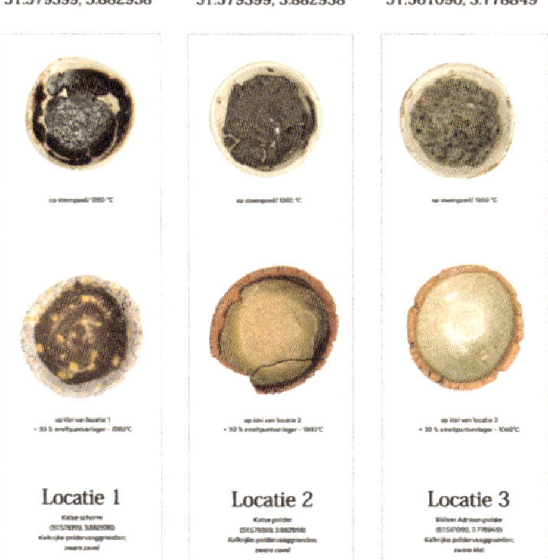

Rink decided to experiment further with the material. She tested different kiln temperatures and also began to make glazes from the unfiltered clay.

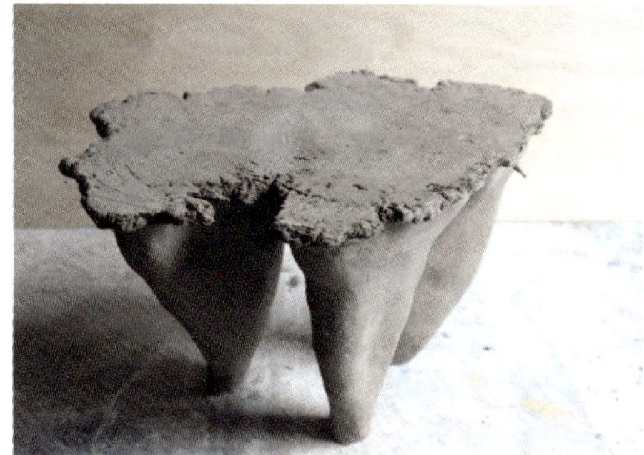

From the question of what she could do with all her findings, besides making a book, and from her need to make something concrete, she continued to search for form.

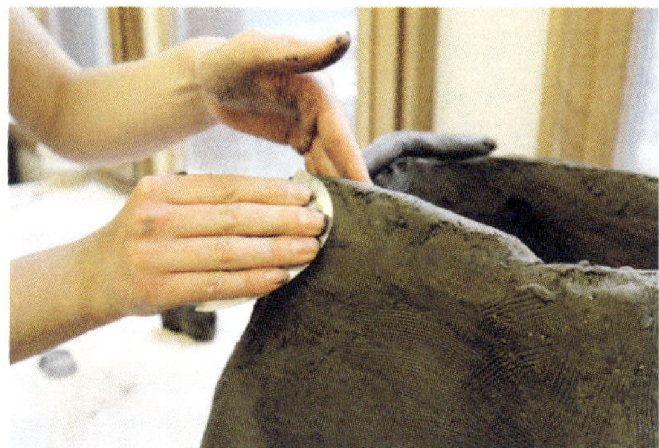

Rink's search for form was a real collaboration with the material. She wanted to use it without losing its roughness.

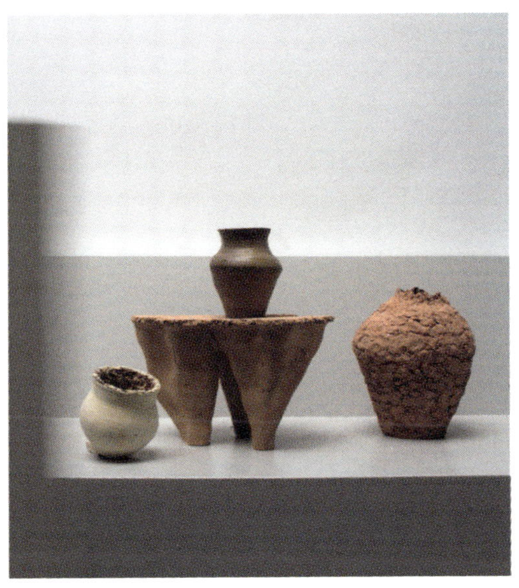

During her graduation, Rink exhibited a collection
of objects.

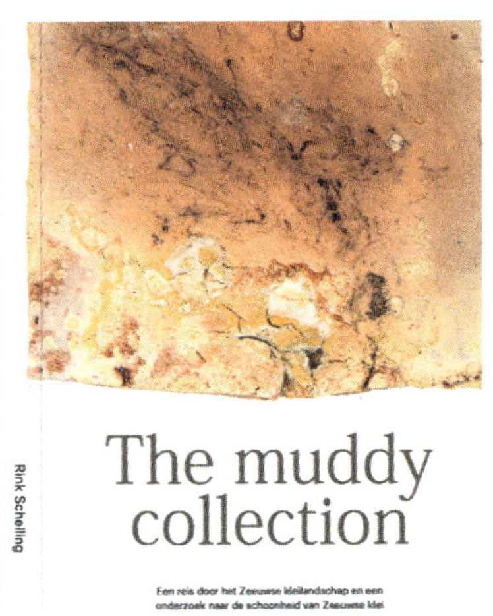

The material research was shared in a
book.

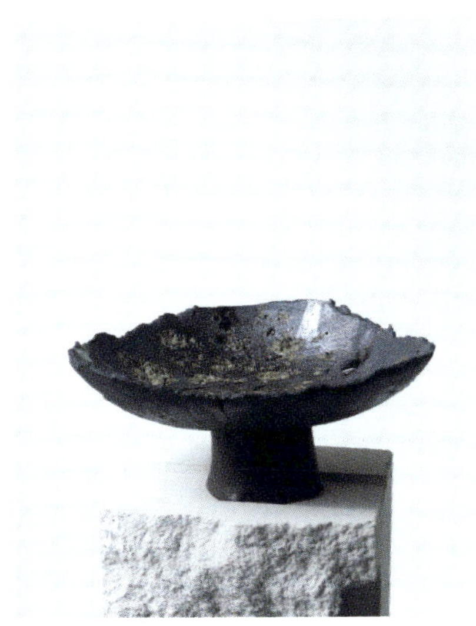

Since her graduation, Rink continues to
build on her research project.

#studying clay
#photographing the process
#mapping the area
#talking with an expert
#fieldtrip with a geologist
#experimenting with clay
#making samples
#classifying samles
#defining a concept
#tests with kiln temperatures
#shaping the material
#exhibiting objects
#producing a book
#experimenting with new glazes

What is out there?

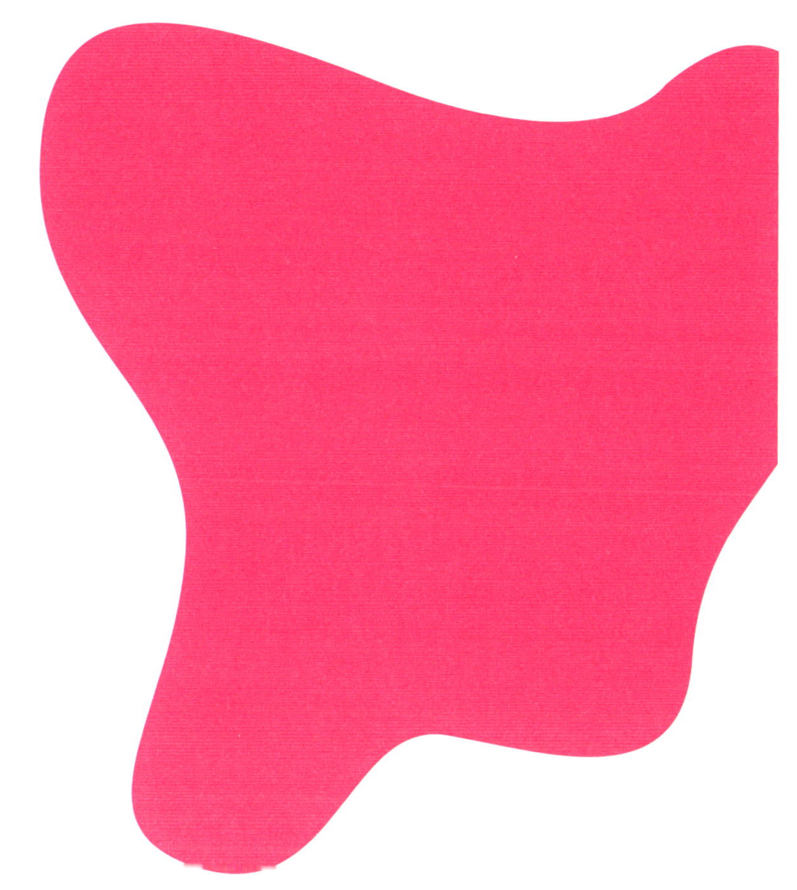

Researching the context of your topic requires valuable sources. There are many different types of sources, both human and non-human, physical and digital, textual, visual and intangible. You can study the work of artists, writers and academics, whether in written form, such as books and articles, or in audiovisual or artistic media.

To understand the context, you might also talk to experts in your field or others who specialise in your subject. Or you can explore the archives, in person or online.

It's also important to consider the social context. What is the bigger picture? What will you need to do to understand it?

Research of context lets you:
> *retrieve what is already known about your subject;*
> *find out what the open and urgent questions are;*
> *get inspired by other artists or designers;*
> *understand the environment in which you work;*
> *learn from specialists and experts;*
> *identify your own perspective and position;*
> *recognise biases and preconceptions.*

album
animation
cartoon
code
dataset
documentary
exhibition
film
historical record
illustration
information graphic
interview
lecture
lyrics
manifesto
memoir
Netflix series
news article
novel
podcast
poem
policy report
review
short story
social media post
song
soundscape
theoretical paper
vlog
workshop

Finding good sources can be daunting. You've probably tried an online search, and chances are you were either overwhelmed by the number of results or disappointed by not finding anything really useful.

A big part of finding good sources is where you look or who you ask. Think of your search for sources not only as a trip to the library, but also as a journey made alongside other people. Don't be afraid to ask around. What works are not to be missed? What online lectures should you listen to? Who should you talk to in person? Who knows all about the history of a place or the relevant people in a network? Once you have found one or two good sources, the expertise of your sparring partner or the reference list at the end of the book or article will point you in the direction of more.

It also helps to experiment with broadening and refining your search terms. Don't stop at the usual search engine – use specific databases, archives and websites where you suspect valuable information can be found. If you've uncovered an audiovisual or artistic source that you like, try describing it with keywords and then use these to search for more.

Don't let preconceptions about academic research hold you back. Anything you find interesting can be used as a starting point for research, as long as you indicate why the source is important to you. You can do this by making an annotated reference list. Note down each source and describe its relevance to your project. What did you see, hear and learn, and what further questions does the source raise? You can relate this to your research question or work more associatively.

To save a lot of frustration later on, keep track of your sources from the outset: note down the name, location and date. Where possible, download online sources. You never know when they will disappear.

What got you interested in a topic – a news item, a film, an exhibition, a song, a podcast? Think of that as your first source.

Are your sources all of the same type, found in the same place or of a similar origin? In that case, how can you diversify your source list?

How does the medium or format affect the information?

Human sources are an important part of research of context. Getting to know the constellation of artists, designers, peers, academics and other researchers in the field of your research subject will help you to contextualise and reflect on what you're doing. These people may have expertise in material or participatory processes, or valuable experiential, artistic or academic knowledge in a field related to your topic.

Mapping people and their practices is a way of understanding your own position within a broader network of knowledge and people. How do you relate to a particular way of working, to certain outputs, publications or audiences? Articulating what you want to add to the field is part of getting to know current practices.

How can you expand your map of a network in different directions?

Looking at your own position, can you articulate what you (want to) bring to existing practices?

What route do you need to take through a network to get to a certain place?

position yourself

> Explore the field in which you work. This could be a particular subject, medium or discipline, or an organisation or client.

> Dive into the history and browse the documents, photos and graphics you encounter.

> Look for experts who have created insightful work, products or knowledge related to your research topic(s).

> Ask peers about their inspirations and who they consider to be knowledgeable in the field or on the topic at hand.

> Visualise all the material you have collected, whether on a wall or on a digital mood board.

> Place yourself on the map: what are your goals and ambitions for this project? How do you see (or want to see) your own position in the field?

Talking to an experienced professional can be very helpful in the research process. An expert can give insight into your question, and each dialogue can deepen your reflections on the subject. In this way you will gain more in-depth knowledge, artistic insight or experiential understanding of a topic.

What do you want to know and how do you aim to get there?

What can only this expert tell you? Do you have enough information to ask the right questions?

Can you offer something in return for picking their minds?

exchange

> Analyse the work of artists, designers, writers and others who inspire you. Why do they speak to you and what can you learn from them?

> Be frank about your own limitations. What don't you know or can't you do? Who could help you with this? Can you arrange a meeting with that person?

> Formulate questions about the topic, approach or viewpoint in which your interlocutor has expertise. Be aware of how your work or research relates to theirs.

> Think about how to design the encounter. Will you have a question-and-answer session? Do you bring tangible work to the table? Do you meet in a specific place? What are you offering in return?

> Talking to experts or other knowledgeable people can begin to look like participatory research. Take into account ethical considerations, as always when involving other people.

So you've found a ton of sources. What do you do now?

Research of context is not about finding as much information as possible – the most important thing is to have sources that are valuable to your project.

You can evaluate your sources vertically, looking for a deeper understanding of your subject, and horizontally, looking to broaden your scope. As your insight grows, you refine your questions and your search. A valuable source may tell you something that opens new avenues of inquiry or that closes old ones. This in turn helps you find other, more specific sources, whether it's a book or another artist working on the same theme.

But research of context also means trying to understand the theme or social issue you are working on from a multi-faceted point of view. There's never just one interpretation, one story, one history. That's why it's important to look for different perspectives and voices, whether they're artists, writers or theorists. In this way, you can bring different sources into conversation with each other and with your own voice.

How do you know when you know enough?

There will always be more to read, learn and discover. But provided your topic is specific enough, there will come a time when additional sources don't really tell you anything new about the context but mostly provide more of the same information and examples. There's no way of knowing exactly when this will happen, and often you'll be on a deadline that doesn't allow you to go that far. Rest assured that the point of saturation is somewhere ahead of you.

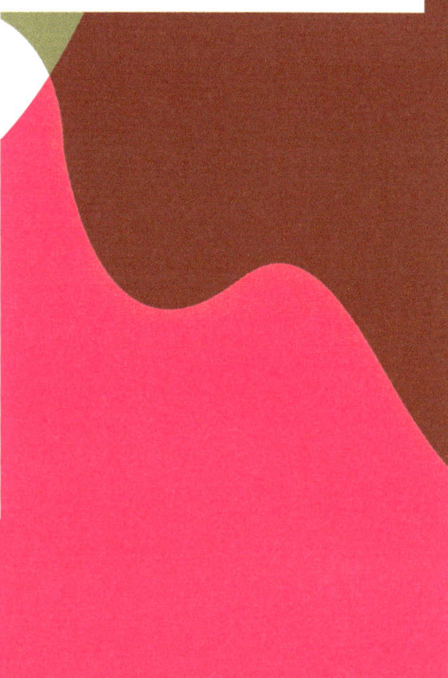

go in-depth

> Consider the diversity of what you have found. In addition to formats and media, consider the diversity of gender, ethnicity and historical period. Voices or imaginations from different backgrounds and contexts are essential for going in-depth. Referencing is a political act; it's important to think about who is being named. A diverse approach will always strengthen your research.

> Go against the grain. Ask yourself what the 'bad' examples or counterpoints to your own ideas or the public opinion might be. Can you find someone who says the opposite of what you tend to think? How do different points of view contradict or complement each other? We're all bound to have blind spots, just like history, culture and society do.

> Make sure it is trustworthy. If you are relying on a source, you want to be able to trust it. Find out who the author is and what their credentials are. Who published the information and for what purpose? How old is it and are there references that allow you to verify the data?

> Make sure it's not fake. In the age of generated content and fake news, you can't trust a source at first glance. Online AI text and image detectors can do some of the work, but not all. Would it affect your argument if AI was actually used to create your source? If so, can you find another source to use instead?

> Question the content critically. After spending some time with the source, try to summarise the content. You can use critical reading and visual analysis tools. Does it answer your question? Why or why not? Does it refute what you have already found or does it raise new questions? Pay attention to the visual aspects and to sound and non-verbal communication. How does it speak to you on an experiential, emotional or physical level?

A well-chosen quote will enliven your work with other voices. Perhaps someone has said something beautiful or pithy that can't be better put. Perhaps you want to give an example of a particular way of thinking or writing. A quote can act as a piece of evidence in your argument or provide a starting point, a summary or a conclusion. The act of quoting shows that you know what you're talking about and that you've done the work. But it can also add inspiration or a touch of elegance to your research documentation.

There can be many reasons for embedding sources in your research presentation and doing so always requires attention and precision. A direct quotation is a verbatim account of what someone has said or written and should be placed in quotation marks and referenced. Paraphrasing is another way of presenting sources in your work. To paraphrase, you repeat what has been said in your own words and make clear where you got your information from.

Consider how you can do justice to your sources in your use of quotations. Be careful not to quote selectively!

If you read your quotes closely, are you certain you understand the meaning of each word?

Can you paraphrase a given quote in your own words or translate it into another language? Does the meaning change?

If you were an outsider to your research presentation, could you trace all sources back to... the source?

Who owns the copyright to an Instagram story or social media post?

Of course, depending on the medium in which you are making your research public, visuals can also be included in your work, as can audio or video clips. Such sources make your presentation attractive and persuasive. Let the reader or viewer see for themselves what you have found. Whether it's a quote or an image, it's important not just to copy a source into your presentation, but to articulate what it means to you and how it relates to your question. Embedding means providing a context for the source. By mentioning names and titles, but also by telling or showing the role it plays in your research.

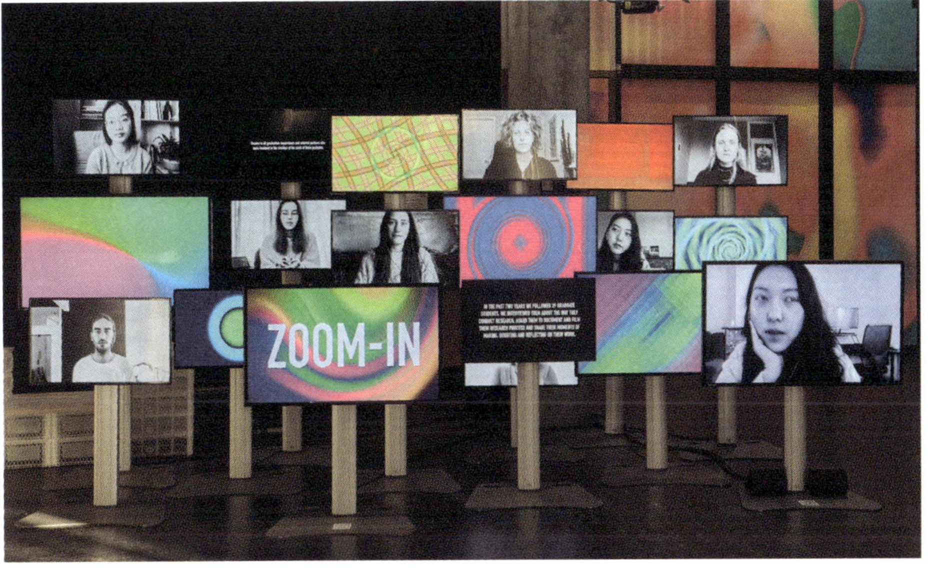

Research Station | *Zoom In* | As part of the WdKA *Zoom In* research project, students were filmed as they researched their graduation projects. These films were screened during the Graduation Festival 2021.

The devil is in the detail.

You don't want to risk plagiarism or unfair use of the work of other artists or researchers. This is why it is important to be careful about referencing and crediting your sources.

It is essential to make sure that you are allowed to copy, reprint or exhibit visual and other material. It is usually not a problem to quote a short piece of text. Check the licences of the images you want to use, such as Creative Commons or free culture licences, and always credit where you found them. You can use a reverse image search to find the source of graphics, paintings or photographs. The results are often accompanied by valuable information.

Citation means that the reader or viewer can find the exact wording or audio-visual material when they look up the source themselves. Citation managers such as Zotero and EasyBib allow you to keep track of your (textual) sources and generate a reference list in the format of your choice, such as MLA, APA or Chicago style. You can find comprehensive guides to these different referencing styles online. The same goes for referencing interviews with experts or archival documents.

Try to be consistent and generous in your referencing practice. Referencing is above all an act of sharing and acknowledging the work of others who have gone before you.

[+] *A source can be textual, visual, oral, scientific, popular, artistic, academic, online, printed, digital, analogue, human, non-human, natural, artificial, etc.*

[+] *Sources can lead to new and different insights. Any source can be valuable if you describe its relevance to your question.*

[+] *Traceability is an act of kindness to the source and to the reader.*

What is out there?

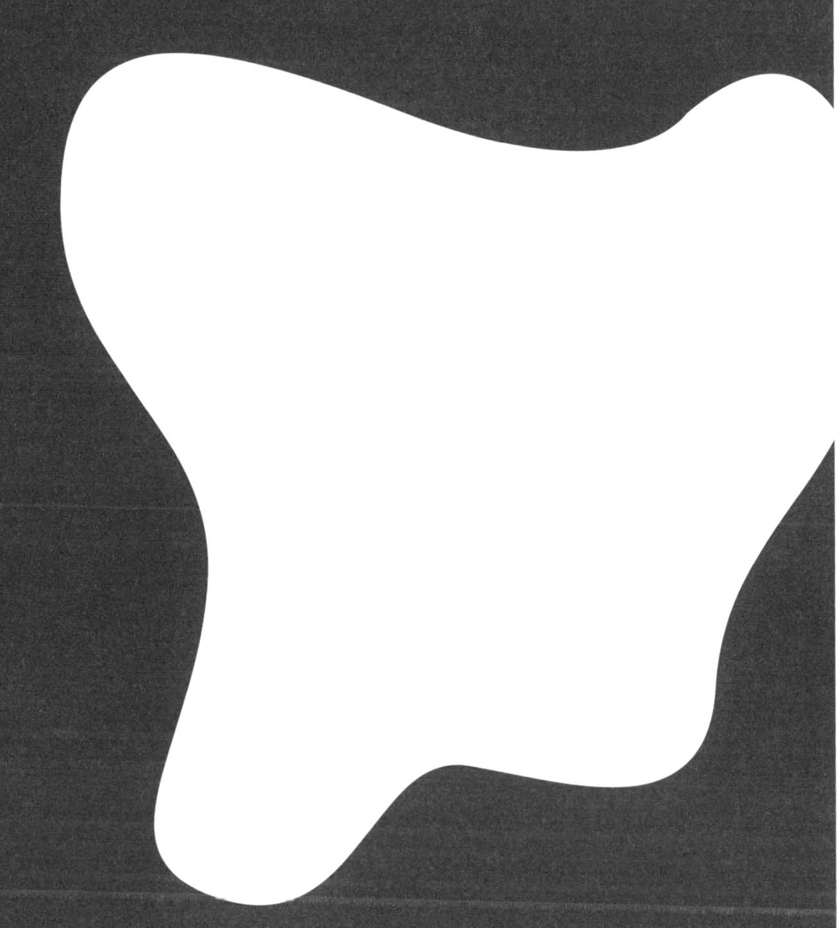

Victoria McGuire | *The Electronic Membrane* | 2023 | Graduation research, BA Fashion Design, WdKA

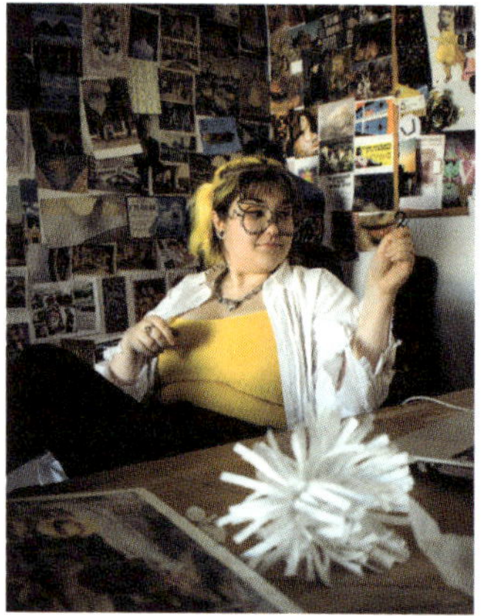

Victoria McGuire is a fashion designer who graduated in 2023 with a research on AI and the future of men's suits.

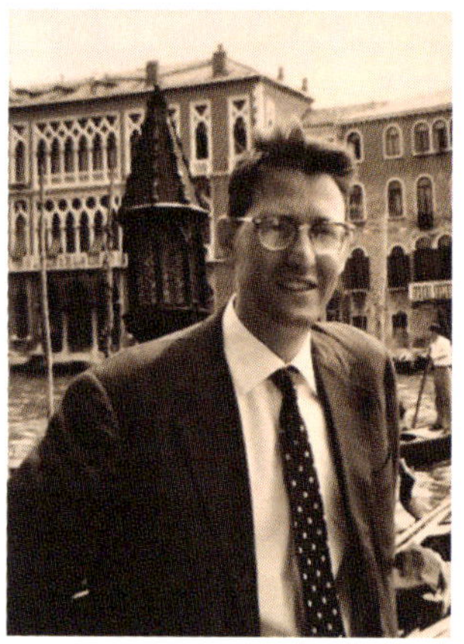

Victoria's love for men's suits inspired her to create a suit for the current generation that normally wears streetwear. In her final year she combined this with her curiosity about the role of AI in design.

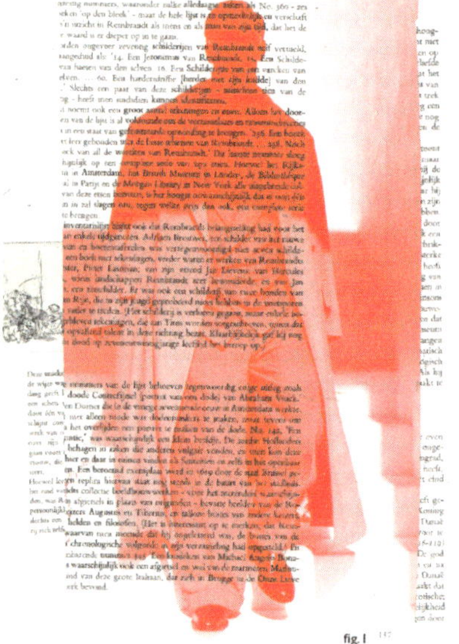

Victoria started by writing a manifesto of everything she wanted to do and that she had already done.

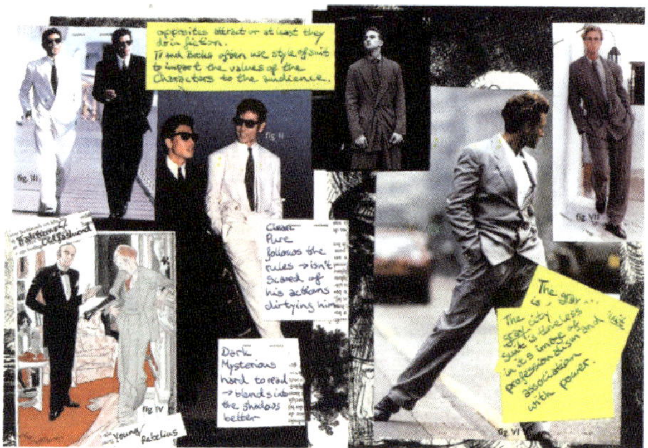

She collected information about suiting, read a lot of sources, especially historical ones, and then curated and analysed her material.

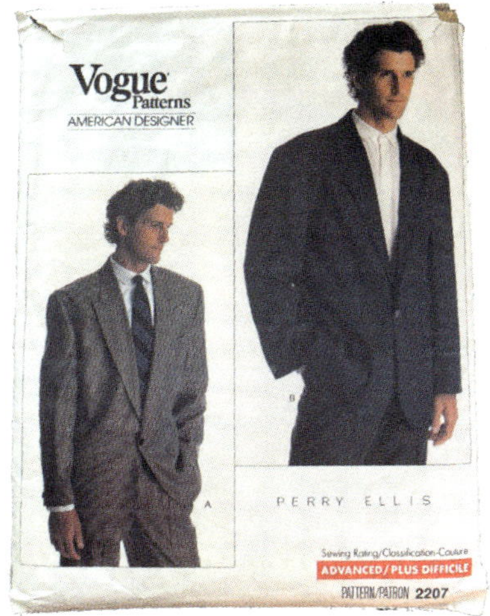
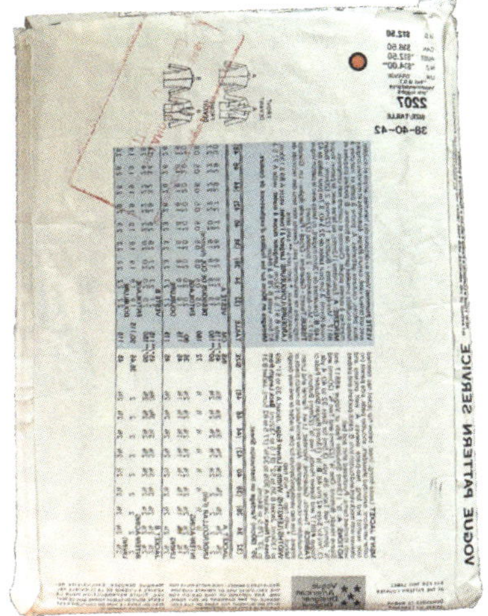

Victoria searched the internet and found an original pattern for a men's suit by Perry Ellis, a designer from the 1980s. She made the suit from the pattern and converted the pattern into a digital file.

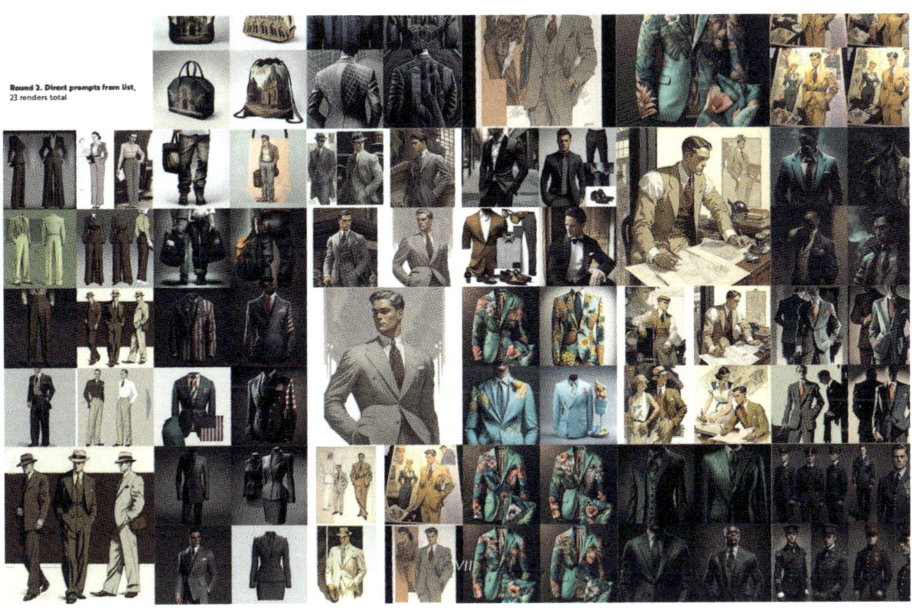

Victoria then tried out various AI programs and chose one she was comfortable with.

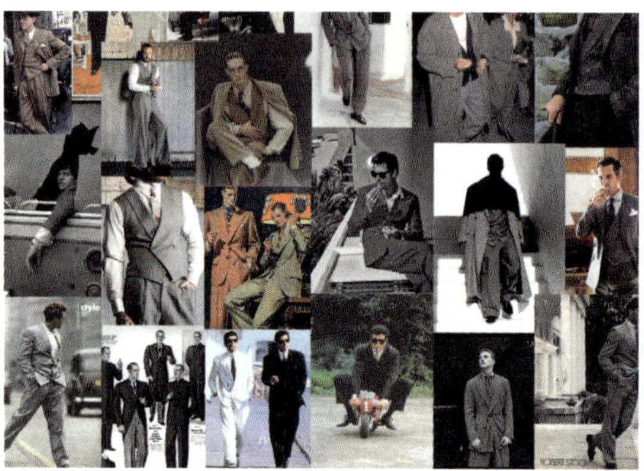

Victoria collected many images of men's suits using Pinterest and other sources, then selected eight images and categorised them.

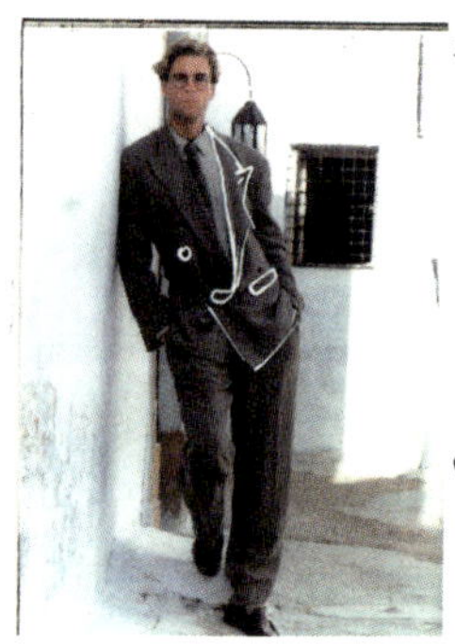

She analysed the data from the selected images, using the strategies of pairing and comparing. She added words to the images to create prompts and used them to generate the AI images.

First list of search terms

Full prompts 11	Fabric pattern reflected in background Summer safbric suit American-Italian suit Gray 90's suit Suit without suit jacket Relaxed formal wear Pinstriped suit Buisness casual 1920's Green pinstript suit Salmon checkerd suit Juxtaposed traditional vs. playful
Clothing related discriptors 21	Old school dress uniform Handkerchief pocket Rose in button hole Pleated pants Herringbone weave Cuffed trousers Overcoat Wide fit Draped Wide suit pants Matching suit and tie Welt pockets Double welt pockets Oxford bags Placed collar Shoal collar Sleeve garters Pinstripes Streight leg wide trousers Flapp pockets Wight suit
Other dicriptors 16	Obscured face Black & wight Half light half dark composition Italoamerican 1930's Pop of color Strong lines Colors Complementary colors 1930's upercalss Double act Old vs new Pure Defined character Police Detective
Enviroment 6	Palms Meditaranian city background Smokers club Retro technologie Japan 1980's Illustration to real
Mood 8	Suave Relaxed pose Rebellious Live action Sunglasses at night Mysterius Dark Clean

To go further, Victoria immersed herself in references on creating prompts and developed a system for writing new prompts, starting with a knowledge-based description of the image.

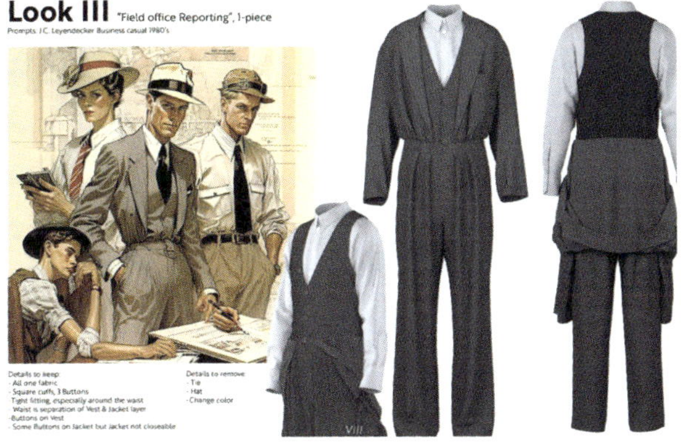

Victoria made a selection of the AI generated images. This selection formed the basis of eight new designs for men's suits, four of which she made.

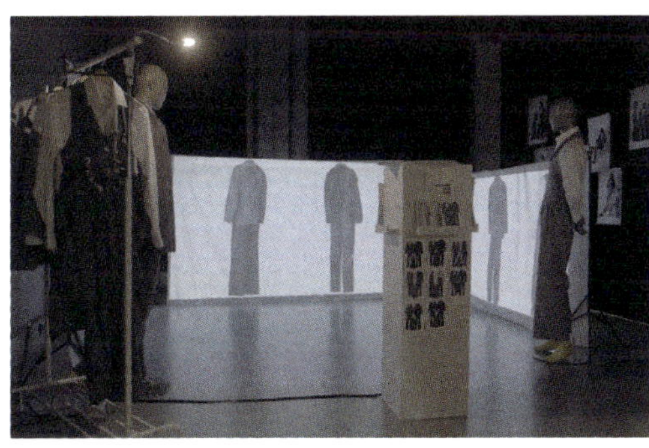

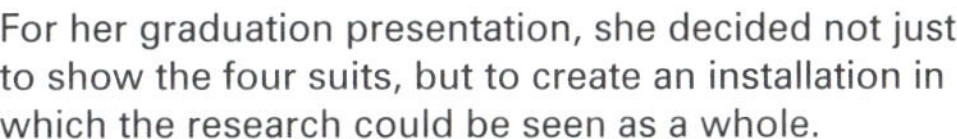

For her graduation presentation, she decided not just to show the four suits, but to create an installation in which the research could be seen as a whole.

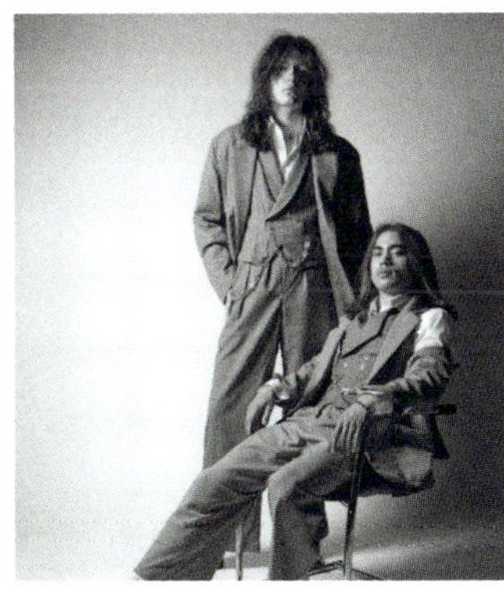

The suits are now being worn, some individualised. They are an answer to the question of designing the simplest possible suit. As they are worn, the deeper meaning of Victoria's research will slowly disappear.

#AI-generated design
#writing a manifesto
#collecting information
#analysing data
#remaking an existing pattern
#researching systems
#categorising images
#describing images
#making prompts
#selecting outcomes
#designing a collection
#curating material
#making an installation
#altering designs for users

Who can put me to the test?

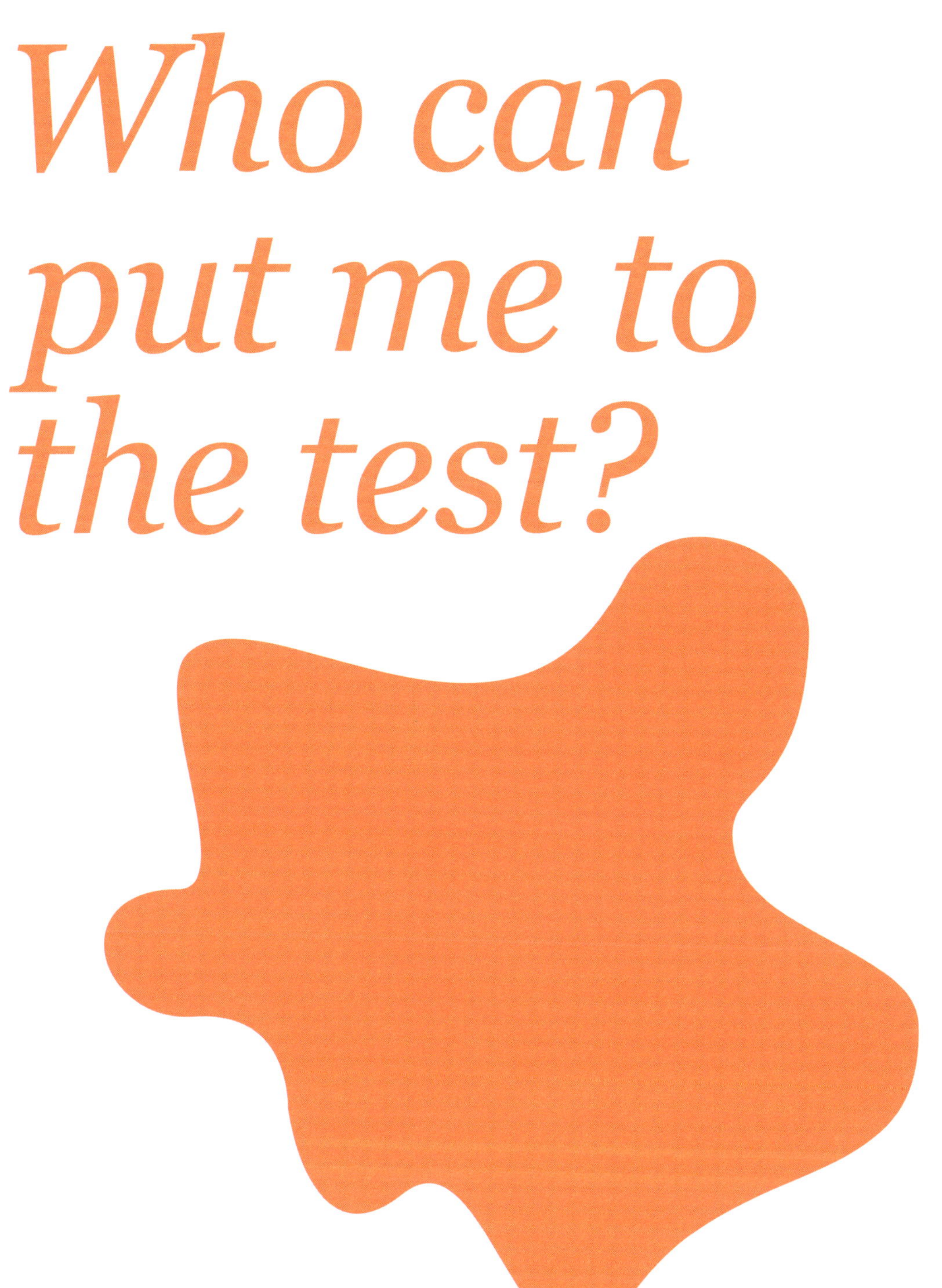

'Nothing about us without us.' It could be an adage for participatory practices in art and design research, as it is in political action. In any research project it is always advisable to involve others, but especially when the topic concerns a group of people. The fact is that you can't know everything about anything (otherwise you wouldn't need to do research), and other people are troves of valuable information the types of which can't be gleaned from books.

Something is bound to happen when you get together with others. People are inherently unpredictable, and working with them means making room for the unexpected – an important thing in art and design. You are forced to put your own ego aside and think about other people's perspectives. Interacting with other people will inevitably burst your bubble and perhaps push you out of your comfort zone. A little interpersonal friction goes a long way in challenging your existing ideas and assumptions.

People bring their own experience to the table. Experiences they have as individuals and in groups, and those that unfold as you interact with them. Sometimes you have a clear objective when you ask others for their participation, for example if you ask them to test or prototype. In other cases, involving others is about the process rather than the outcome. About sharing, making connections and creating togetherness rather than what is concluded at the end.

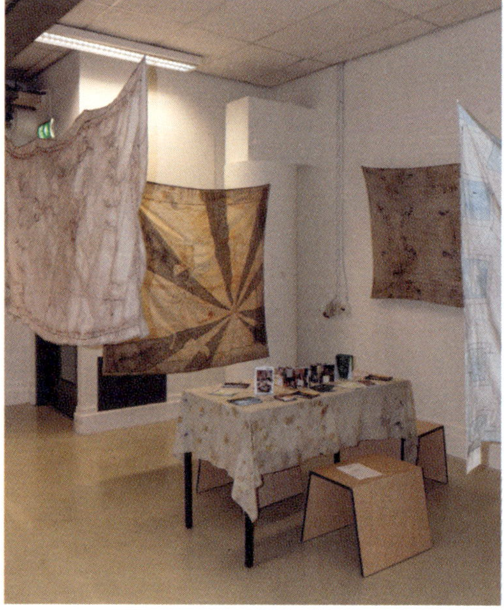

Katayun Taraporevala | *Queer Migrants Eating* | 2024 | Graduation project, BA (de)Fine Arts, WdKA | Katayun wanted to recreate the communal eating experiences she valued as a member of the Parsy community in India. She researched communal eating as a means to build a community for queer migrants. She created personalised, naturally dyed tablecloths with embroidered designs that served as a thank you to her queer migrant family and symbolised the bond they had formed through shared experiences and meals.

Participatory research is about working with people. They may be collaborators in a project, they may have valuable experience or they may be part of a particular audience. The act of making can be closely linked to participatory research, in particular in art and design practices. Interactive designs, co-creation and interdisciplinary processes combine creative methods with more 'traditional' ones such as interviewing and observation. You can use tangible materials to bring out everyone's knowledge, such as conversation pieces, cultural probes or prototypes. You can work collaboratively and non-hierarchically.

Working with others will strengthen your research, but also requires ethical consideration. What do you offer your participants in return? How can you create a valuable experience for your participants in addition to gaining the knowledge or results you need?

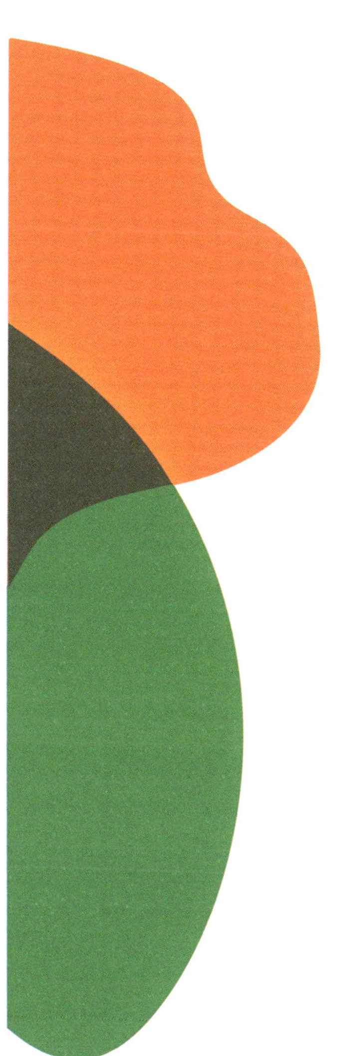

Involving others in your research project will let you:
> *learn from other people's stories and experiences;*
> *add to the information you've found in ways you can't imagine yourself;*
> *test an application, a design, an object, a workshop or a show;*
> *put yourself in a new environment and listen;*
> *meet new people and have fun;*
> *engage with the unexpected.*

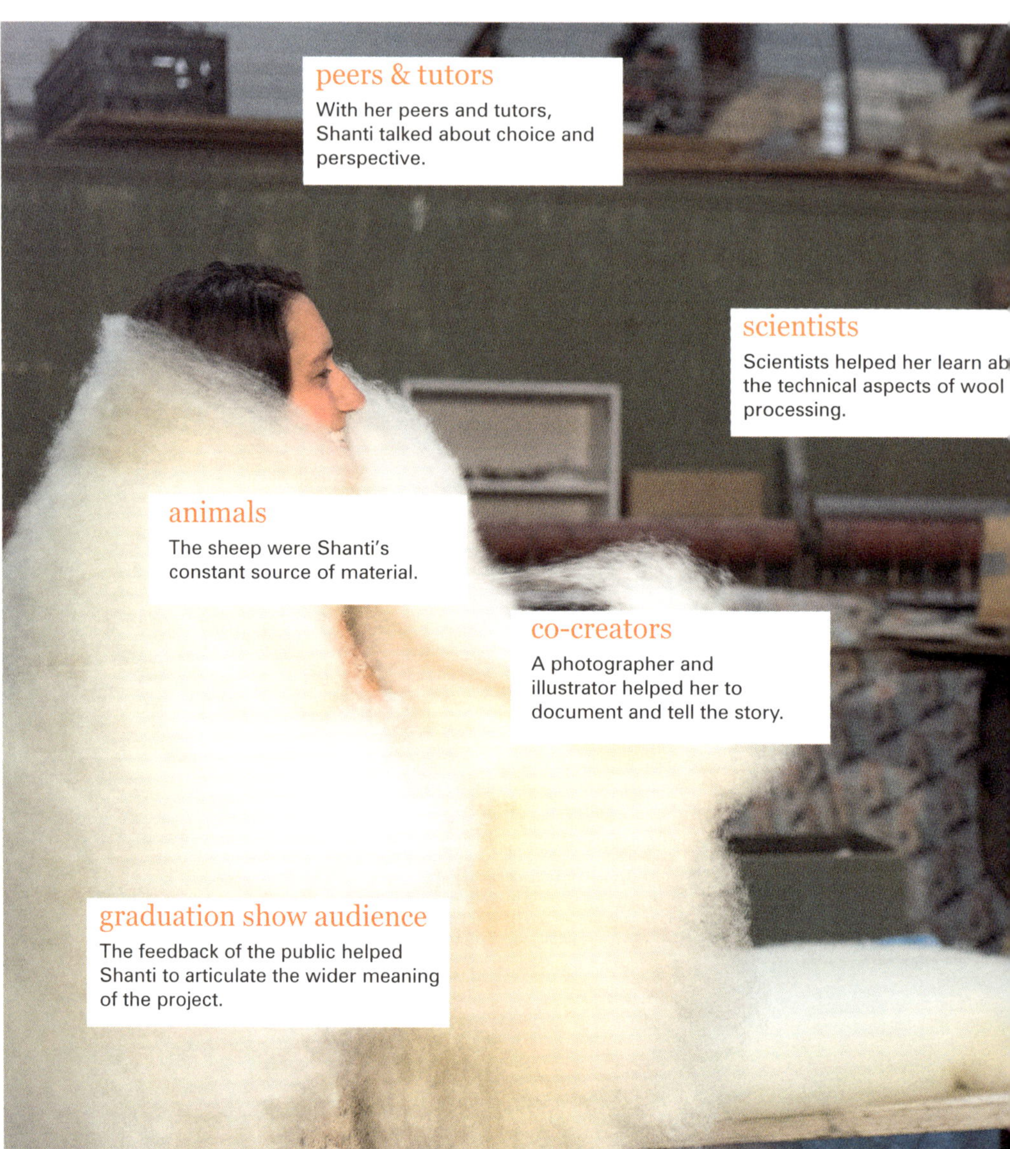

Shanti Versnel | *Project Skiep* | 2021 | Graduation research, BA Product Design, WdKA

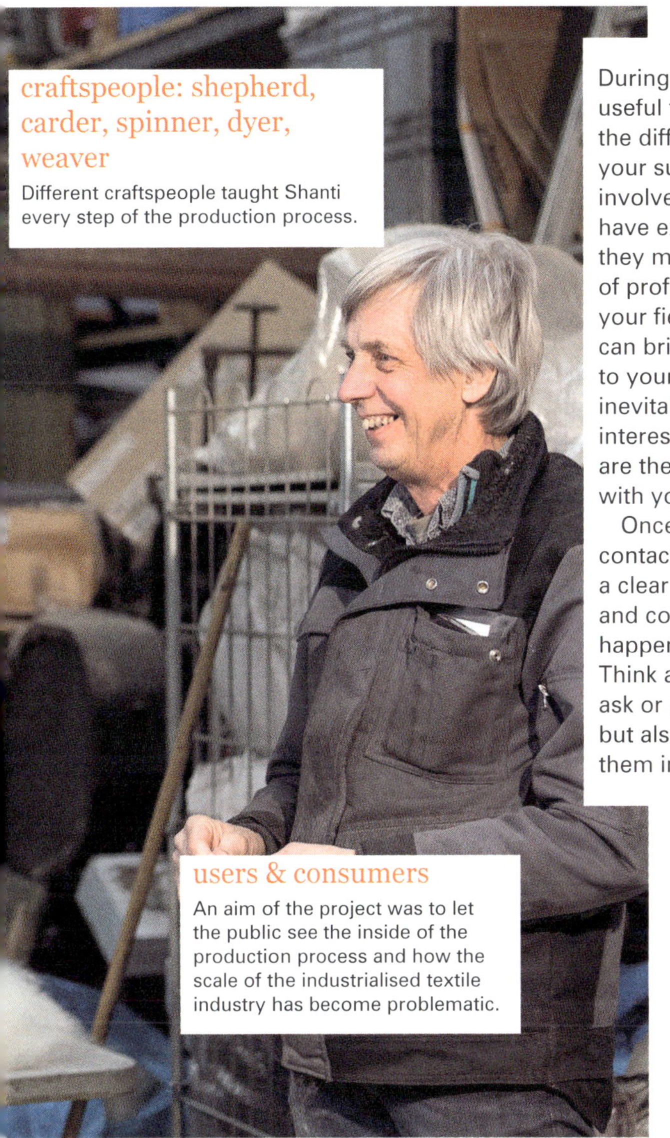

During your research it's useful to get an overview of the different people related to your subject. The people you involve in your project may have experience in the topic, they may be a defined group of professionals working in your field of interest or they can bring unexpected insights to your project. Who will you inevitably work with? Who is interesting to work with? And are they interested in working with you?

Once you have made contact, you need to set up a clear process and define and communicate what will happen in the exchange. Think about what you want to ask or get from each of them, but also what you can offer them in return.

For *Project Skiep* Shanti spent a week cycling around the province of Friesland, visiting people at every stage of the wool production process. She researched the skills and knowledge of the craftspeople involved in the process from raw material to finished product. She documented the journey in a book.

More and more, research in the arts and design is done collaboratively. You work with others collectively, even if one of you is ultimately in charge. You might be working with other artists or designers, with researchers from other disciplines, or with experts in the field, volunteer participants, neighbours, friends, etc.

Collaborating with others is a way of incorporating dialogue and multiple perspectives into the project inherently. It allows you to learn and get to know each other in a deep and personal way. It is also fun to work with others, given that research can sometimes be a lonely affair.

There are many aspects to consider when beginning or joining a collaborative project. In a research setting, it is particularly important to consider roles and hierarchies, agreements on how to work together, and the types of knowledge that will be created.

What are your own implicit and explicit roles?

What do they allow you to do, or not to do?

What comes naturally to you and where could you grow or learn?

Roles and hierarchies should be made explicit whenever you work together. Often they can be embodied and can run along lines of gender or ethnicity. If you don't make make an effort to make them explicit, implicit power relations may take over.

Don't be afraid to talk about power, privilege and capacity. What can each person contribute? Not everyone has the same skills or can invest the same amount of time and energy. Make space for differences, but also for growth. Not everyone has to do the same thing all the time if you share and learn from one another.

Clear agreements will open space for co-creation and build trust between participants. Goals, concepts, media and public can all be part of the initial discussion, as can expectations, wishes and fears. But don't forget to talk about things like budget, administration, time management and planning as well. It is also important to pay attention to the language used and how things are communicated. Who is responsible for what and how do you check in with each other?

Also think about documentation. Since the process of collaboration is so important, you want to make sure it is carefully documented. Everyone should have a say in the methods, formats and aims of the documentation. The same goes for publication. Is everyone on the same page about where and how the project might be published? How do you keep this conversation going?

Depending on the size of the group and the project, you'll need to invest time and perhaps other resources to get to know each other. A fulfilling experience for everyone cannot be guaranteed in advance, so make sure there is an open space for dialogue. Also think about where people can turn if things go wrong.

The stakes for the collaborators should be clear from the start. They may learn or experience something painful and frustrating, or even relive bad memories. It is very important to mitigate these risks.

New ways of knowing emerge when different disciplines and backgrounds work together. Value what each discipline brings to the table. Multi-, inter- and transdisciplinary projects are important for combining knowledge or weaving new kinds of knowledge. Bringing together different ways of working, making, understanding and thinking is an important way to address complex questions and issues. This requires space and time and an open attitude to each other's knowledge and skills. It can be a long process but it's definitely worth it.

Can you make room for failure and misunderstanding?

How much control do you have over the situation and what do you allow to 'just happen'?

Do you dare to trust the process and listen to your co-creators?

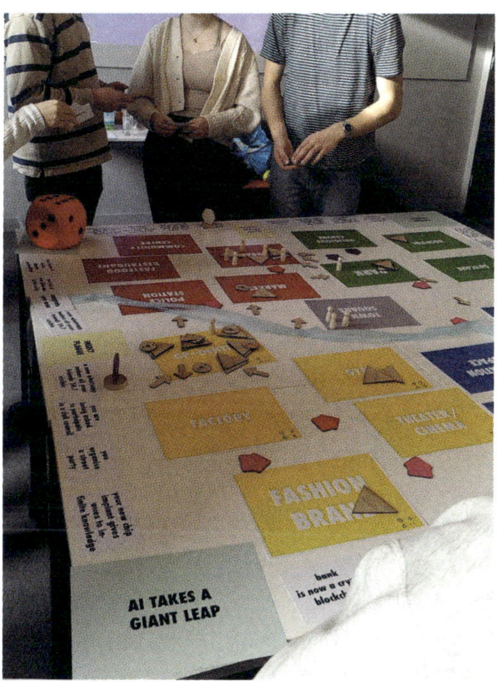

Esther Verhamme | *Polaris: A Simulation Game for Rehearsing Polarisation* | 2024 | Graduation research, MA Master Design, PZI | A design research project on social dynamics between (groups of) people. Esther explored polarisation in different iterations where participants speculated on future scenarios with the use of collective imagination.

Extend the usual methods of participatory research

– such as interview, survey or participant observation – and use tangible objects to guide an interaction in order to have a meaningful exchange with a defined group of participants. This immediately links your actions to research by making and is therefore particularly useful for art and design research.

A designed object or situation can provoke different kinds of responses and exchanges. Unexpected things are likely to happen. As an initiator, you take a certain position and role in the exchange and you should be well prepared. What do you do when things go differently to how you had hoped or expected?

An exchange need not be limited to verbal dialogue, it can also seek an answer based on the sensory experience of the participants. How do you access the knowledge that your participants hold in their hands, hearts or minds? What do they see, hear, taste, smell or feel and how does this relate to their lived experiences and beliefs? Using tangible objects helps to bring out information that might otherwise remain pre-verbal or unconscious.

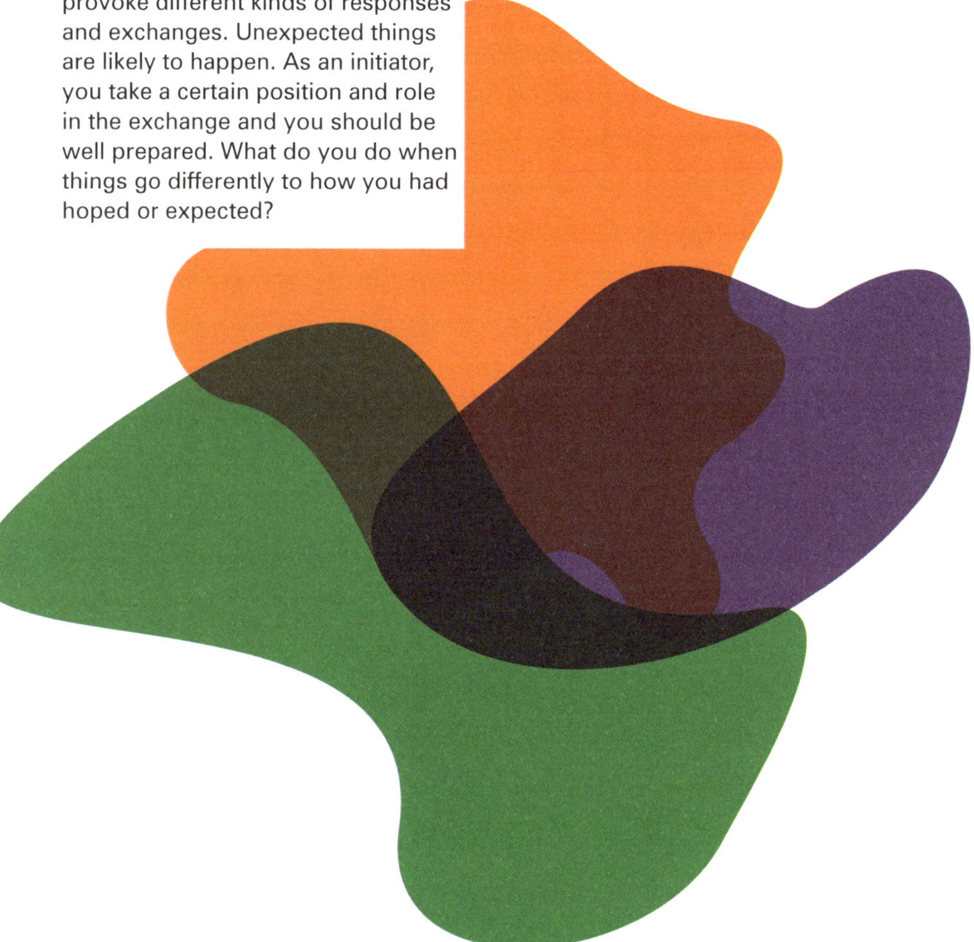

The aim of your action, or the sub-questions you want to address, will determine how you design the encounter. Maybe you want to hear stories about other people's experiences, which can be prompted with pictures or found footage. Or you may want to get feedback on a preliminary design you have made. Are there blind spots or other things you've missed? You can also use a schema to structure your conversation, which can be filled in with keywords or post-its. Tangible objects are a creative way to guide the conversation, rather than just going through a list of questions one by one. In this way, you can avoid being too directive in your conversations or observations and give the other person more space to respond as they wish.
Objects can be used in more provocative ways as well. You may want to evoke primary reactions, challenge established ideas or implicit assumptions. You could use images that depict social problems, but your choice of material could also be more associative, for instance by working with colour or sound. A short scene performed by actors or an improvised dialogue between a pair of researchers could also be seen as a provocation piece.

However, take care of your participants. Don't provoke for the sake of provocation. There is always a chance that you trigger memories or reactions that you could not foresee.

design

Conversation or provocation pieces are tangible objects designed to stimulate interaction. They can be used in combination with prompts or rules and executed in a specific situation.

> First decide what you want to know or what question is central to the session.

> What images, objects or scenarios do you need for you to invite or provoke others to share?

> Do you want to structure the conversation or will you allow it to flow more freely? Try to think about the possible course of the encounter.

> Think about the timing and location of your session. These factors are part of the design of your piece.

> What do you want your participants to do? Will they just talk or will they move, draw, write? Will they interact with each other or just with you?

> How will you document what happens? Don't forget to inform the participants and ask if they agree to be recorded, for example.

> Who will you invite? Think about representation and diversity in your participant group.

> Make room for care and ethics in your design.

- [+] *Who are 'they' and who are 'we'? And who are you in relation to them?*

- [+] *A conversation is like a work of art – give it the attention it needs.*

- [+] *Different groups - different wants - different needs.*

- [ ]

- [ ]

- [ ]

Who can put me to the test?

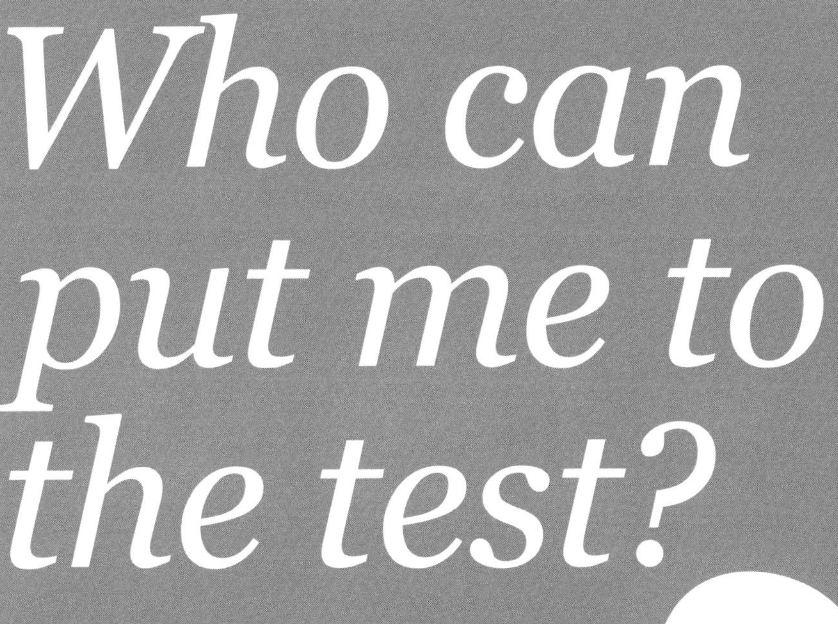

Remty Elenga and Myung Feyen graduated with a collaborative research project on how arts education can help young people to get in touch with themselves and others. They carried out the research at two different schools: ISK, the International Transition Class, where students aged 12-18 from all parts of the world are educated while learning Dutch, in order for them to go on to regular education. And a Havo secondary school with a specialisation in theatre.

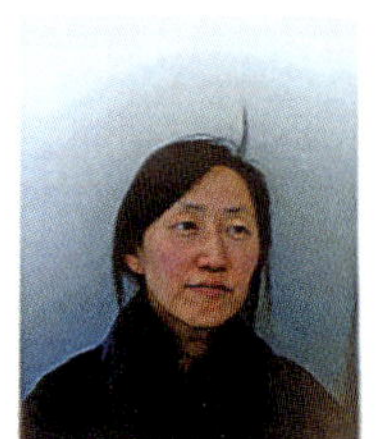

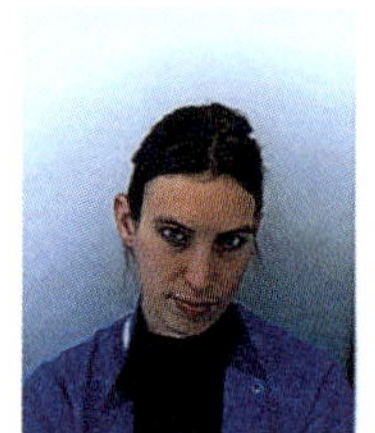

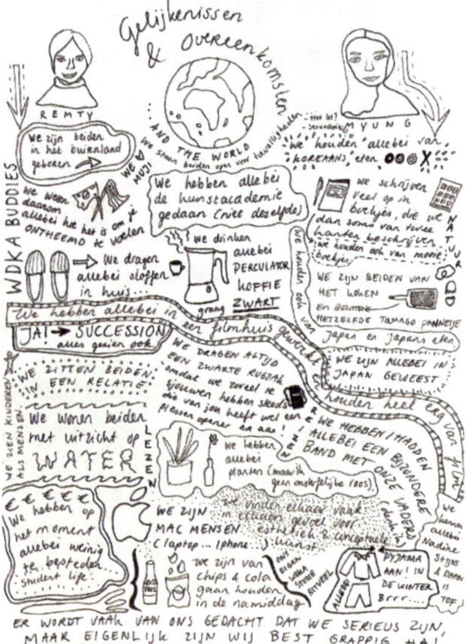

Remty, who was trained as an independent artist, wanted to explore how art education could encourage imagination through experimentation, with her Havo students in mind. Myung, who taught art to a group of newcomers to the Netherlands, saw an opportunity to explore the inner world of young people and translate this into meaningful education. The two of them hadn't collaborated before. Remty decided to write a letter to Myung to find out if Myung would be interested in doing their graduation research together.

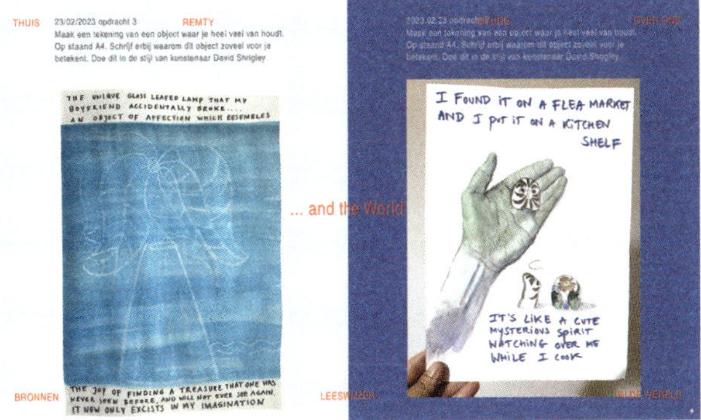

Remty and Myung came up with the idea of not only exchanging letters, but giving each other small creative tasks as well. The aim was to get to know one another better.

In the first weeks of the graduation process, they would focus on these introductory tasks. In weekly meetings they discussed outcomes, next assignments and what they meant for their final project.

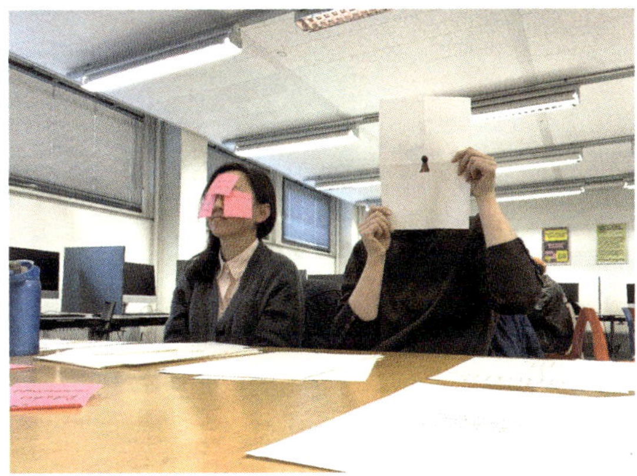

Next to this exchange, Remty and Myung also went through an individual process. Each created their own research blog, where they kept track of their own process and reflections.

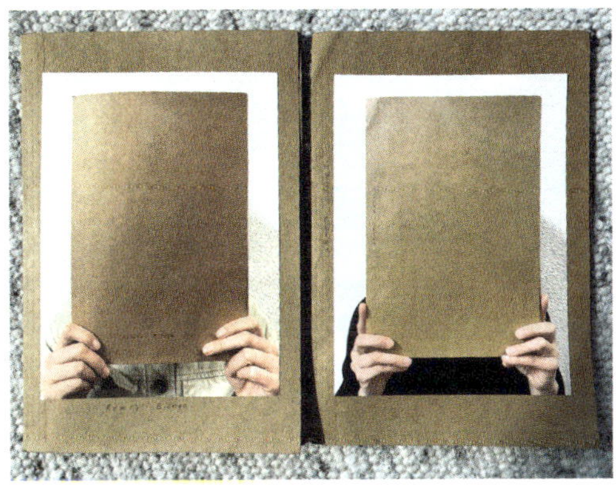

Remty and Myung formulated individual sub-questions and collected relevant sources to contextualise their experiences in their teaching practice. The sources and knowledge were shared on a collaborative blog.

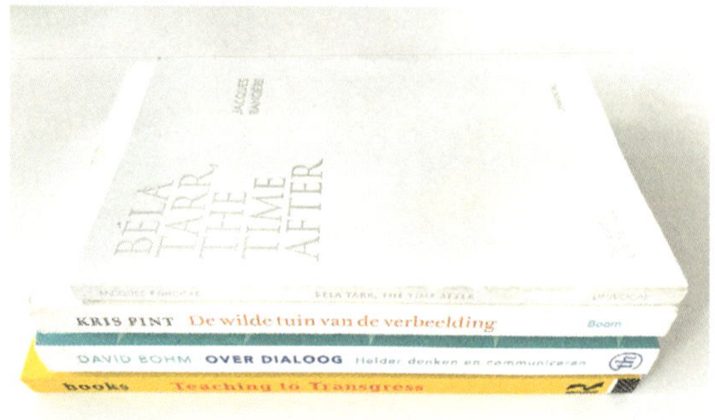

They wanted to translate the process of two individuals meeting and getting to know each other, and at the same time gaining insight into themselves, into an educational product.

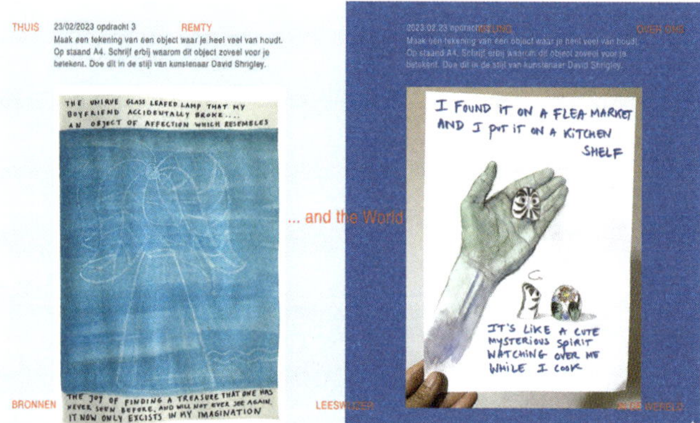

They designed three different lesson series around the topics of getting to know yourself, getting to know the world and getting to know the other.

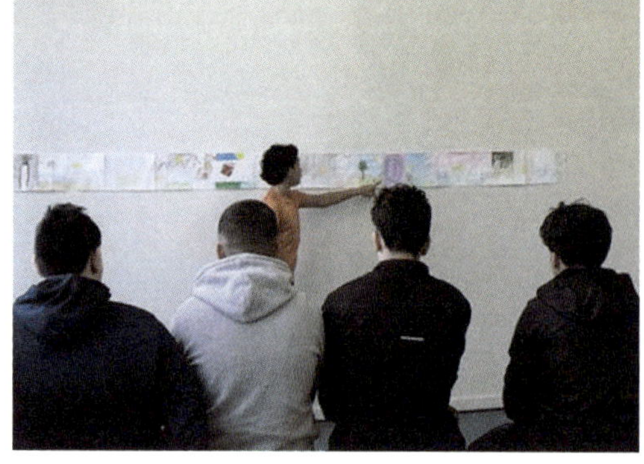

Remty and Myung tested the lessons in their different educational contexts and compared the results. The lessons were adapted where necessary and re-tested with other groups of students. They incorporated the outcomes into their individual research questions.

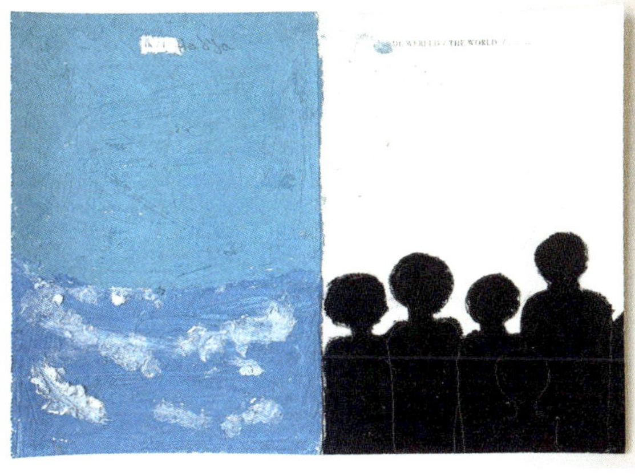

The students' worksheets were as carefully designed as the lesson plans. Their tests showed that carefully designed worksheets gave students extra motivation to work on the assignments.

IK EN DE WERELD

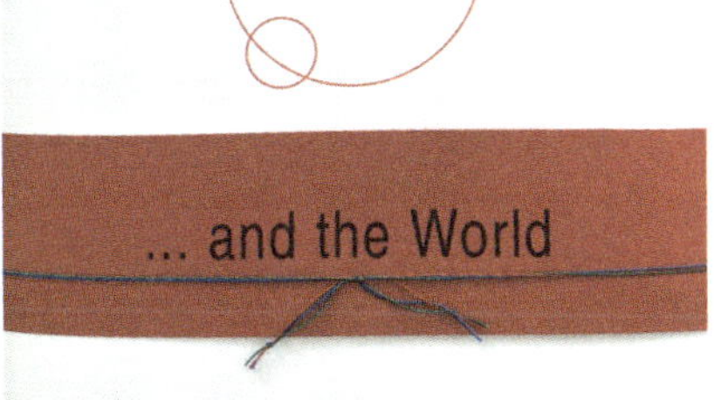

In addition to a physical package containing all the teaching materials, Remty and Myung published online the assignments they gave each other, their research on the context, the teaching materials and the products of their students. They also published their correspondence under the name *Hersenspinsels* (*Braindumps*).

#meeting
#setting up a collaboration
#writing
#giving each other tasks
#discussing results
#joint documentation
#individual research blog
#reading sources
#sharing sources
#making lessons
#teaching
#comparing results
#re-designing lessons
#testing lessons in other
  groups
#designing worksheets
#developing a website
#designing a teaching package

Why do I do what I do?

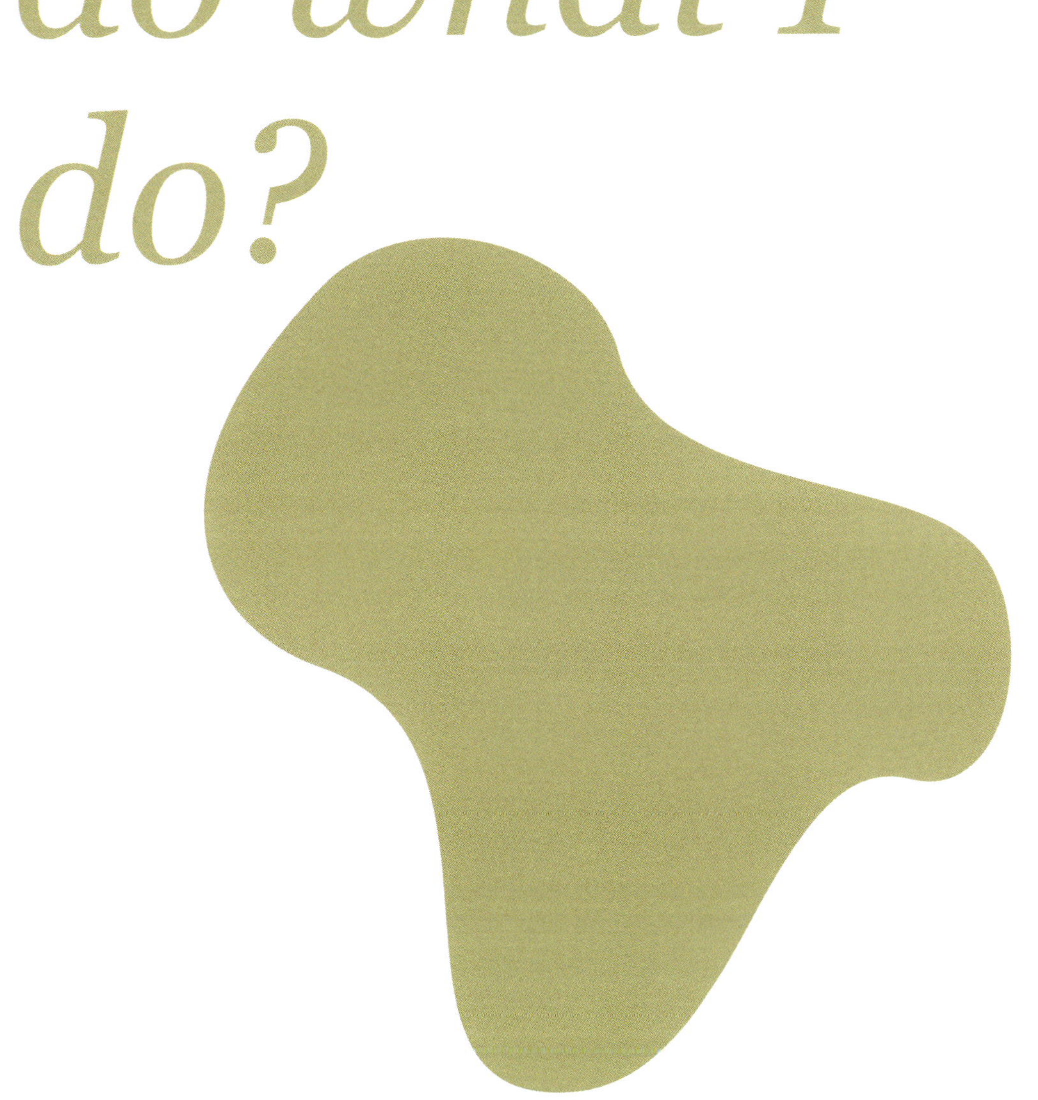

Reflection is at the heart of every research project.

From choosing a topic, methodology or documentation structure, to analysing observations, experiments, other (material) data and deciding on next steps. One's own position and perspective requires constant reflection as well.

While artists and designers are used to doing a lot of reflection on their work and its relation to who they are, here we zoom in on what it means to reflect specifically on research.

As a researcher, you are not a neutral onlooker

collecting data and producing objective knowledge. You have a particular point of view, shaped by your background, experience and training. Implicit understandings or biases may well shape the way you see the world, even if they aren't intended to.

To ensure the validity and integrity of your research, it is important to reflect critically on your positionality. How has your perspective or outlook developed? How does it relate to the topic of your research? What cultural or historical influences have shaped common understandings of a subject, and what role do your multiple identities play in your own understanding of it? Can you ensure that your preconceptions do not shape or predetermine what you find? You could write a reflective statement on your positionality to gain insight into these questions.

collective reflection
brainstorm
group chat
interview
peer feedback
reading group
Socratic dialogue

personal reflection
diary
ethical review
mapping
notebook
position statement
voice recording

Take time and space to reflect on:
> *your own position and background;*
> *the ethics of your project;*
> *questions and possible answers;*
> *choices and decisions;*
> *how to move from one iteration to the next;*
> *what went well and what didn't;*
> *what you found out and what you still don't know.*

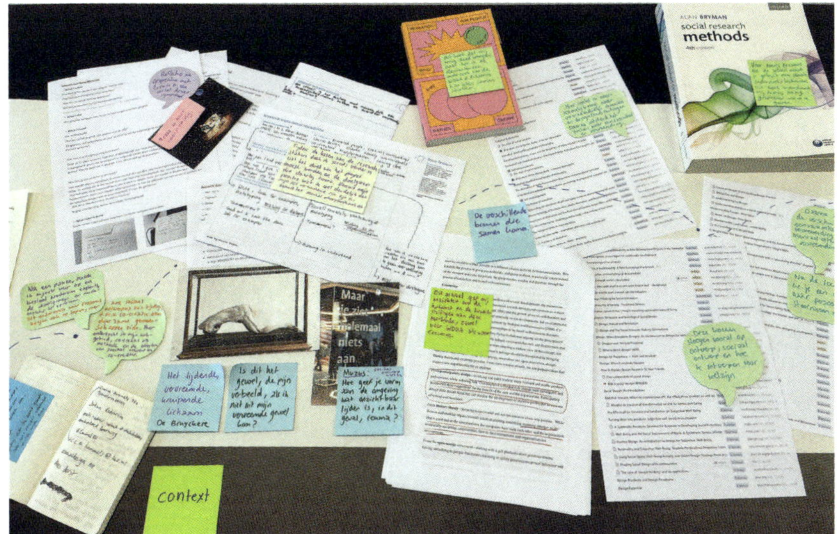

Lianne Vreezen | *The Hidden Alienation* | 2024 | Graduation research, BA dual degree Rotterdam Arts & Sciences Lab (RASL): Transformation Design, WdKA and Arts & Culture Studies, Erasmus University | Research on alienation that combines interviews with experts, workshops and a lot of personal and collective reflection. The documentation feeds directly into the act of making public.

Art and design research is about interacting with the world and with others,

about making a difference or having an impact, whether emotional, experiential or cognitive. With that comes a degree of responsibility. What do you want to achieve? Have you considered the wishes of others? Who gets to decide what is good or even better? An ethical assessment of any research project is recommended to avoid blind spots, to ensure good relations with participants and the public, and to embed the project in a wider context.

Schedule in regular moments for articulated reflection.

By taking a moment daily, weekly or monthly to ask yourself questions and document the answers, you gain a firm grip on the process. It will help you draw conclusions and work towards publication.

It is equally important to reflect on the limitations of what you have found. What do you not know? Not now and maybe never? Stumbling on the limits of (common) knowledge is not a sign of failure, but tells you something meaningful. Not-knowing or non-knowledge could be called a speciality of artistic research.

It's good to formulate goals for a reflection session. Do you want to reflect on the whole process or focus on a particular question? Do you need to make decisions or is it about gaining a deeper understanding? Do you want to plan ahead or see where you're coming from?

Working with others requires careful ethical consideration – especially if your topic relates to personal, physical or even traumatic experiences, issues of identity or social upheaval, or if you want to work with particular groups of people, such as minorities, children or people with disabilities or illnesses.

Doing research is not just about 'getting information', it is also about building relationships and even communities. Even if you are sending out an anonymous survey, it is good to ask yourself what kind of relationship is being built in your actions. What does your project set in motion and how can it be maintained?

More generally, ethics is about doing the right thing in our interactions with others and with the outside world. In recent years, ethics has received increasing attention in art and design research. However, it is still a developing field.

As a researcher, you are committed to certain values. Research integrity is usually described in terms of honesty, accuracy, transparency, independence and responsibility. In art and design there is an invitation to consider other possible values such as reciprocity, mutual care, listening, and 'response-ability'. How can you work towards such relational values in your research? It is bound to be complicated, but also eye-opening.

The planetary perspective is equally important to consider. All research has an ecological impact and affects a wide network of actors, including non-human ones. Mapping these networks and affects can give you insight into the sustainability of your plans and how your actions may be connected to other actors far away. An ecological approach to ethics seeks to understand not only the consequences of your own actions, but also the ripple effect they may move beyond your immediate environment. It also asks how you are affected by others. How does your environment shape, enable or hinder your actions?

What is the relationship between you and the participants?

What are the cultural biases or prejudices that might affect such relations?

Are there any hierarchies that might affect the outcome?

Principles that are applied in research ethics might relate to consent, hierarchy, privacy, copyright and demands on time and effort.

'Informed consent' means that people know they are part of a research project, what the questions and aims of the project are, and what it might mean for them to participate, for example in exhibitions or publications. Participants should give explicit permission for their involvement or the use of their data.

What you ask of people in terms of time and effort should be reasonable. If you are asking someone for a few hours of their time without payment, can you offer something in return, such as valuable experience, knowledge or networking? Keep them informed about the process and your findings.

The question of hierarchy also needs to be examined. What are the power dynamics between you as a researcher and the others in your project? How can you create equality among your collaborators?

The handling of data and participants' privacy is increasingly monitored and regulated. Try not to collect information that you do not need, make sure to store it in a safe place and remove it when you are finished. When publishing, take care that sources remain anonymous unless you have explicit permission to use names and images, for example.

When considering the ethics of your project, try to plan for the unexpected. How will you respond if someone is overcome with emotion? What if someone doesn't want to continue? Can you refer participants somewhere if they have questions or complaints?

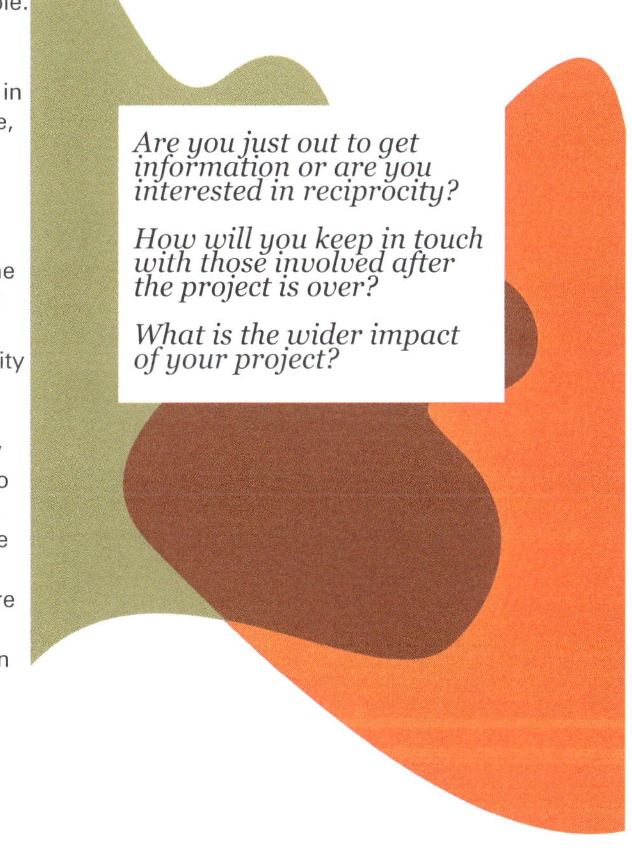

Doing research starts with curiosity. Why is something the way it is? How can you make a difference? What are the conditions for change? But if you are without a more concrete research question, it is going to be hard to navigate the vast expanse of possibilities. For example, if your project is about identity and visual art, where do you start? Asking a question gives direction to your search. Rather than limiting you, it will allow you to dive deeper and go further.

It is often said that formulating a good question is already a kind of answer to a problem. Knowing what to ask requires a sense of the scope of the field – its blank spaces, the interesting nooks and crannies, and the urgencies it holds. This is also why your question may change as your research unfolds. Treat your question as open-ended and fluid, itself subject to investigation and change. Just be sure to document any adaptations and reflections along the way.

Asking a *what* **or** *how* **question** can lead to different approaches. Do you want to explore a social issue? Do you want to know more about a concept or theory? Do you have a question about the process of making? Do you want to find out what it takes to make a difference? Each of these may require its own type of question.

You can use sub-questions to flesh out different aspects of your enquiry. For example, distinguish between your medium, your target audience and your theoretical framework. Think of your questions as a group of critical friends, helping you find your way and providing a map when you get lost.

creative or collaborative topics
media like riso printing or algorithms
methods like protoyping or mapping
roles like art director or social designer

social or cultural topics
circularity
gentrification
public space
queer identity
visual culture
waste systems

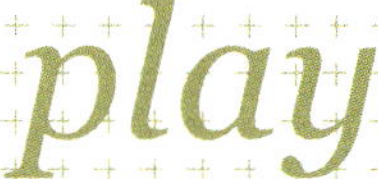

Make reflection on your research question and sub-questions a regular part of your process. You can be playful and experimental in your approach.

> Try to make all the words in your research question as specific as possible. Instead of 'people' say '12-18 year olds living in the city', 'film' might become 'fictionalised short documentary', 'technology' might become 'algorithmic workplace surveillance'.

> Next, make terms such as 'more', 'greater' or 'best' as specific as possible. How will you measure change? It doesn't have to be quantified data. You can also describe or visualise the terms.

> Uncover implicit ideas and perceptions you have about your topic by describing or visualising desired outcomes.

> Divide your research question into sub-questions and plot them on the circle model. Does the question require research by making, participatory research or research of context? Are certain actions missing?

> Reformulate your question and change it from 'what' to 'how' or vice versa. Is the question about theoretical knowledge or about making something? Is it about you or about others? Does it offer an action or a reflection?

> Add and remove the 'I' from your question and see what happens. What are your stakes and curiosities? You can also position yourself in relation to your questions in a visual way.

> Say 'why' five times to go deeper into your question. It works best if someone else asks you. What is your driving force and where do you see the urgency of your research? Why?

A research question is:

> as yet unanswered;
> open-ended (not a yes-or-no question);
> specific, clear and concise;
> a structuring mechanism;
> a work in progress;
> a guide along the way.

How to put into words what you have found?

In the course of your project, you want to build up a constellation of actions and findings that say something about your research question. You may want to make a plausible argument or draw conclusions, however tentative. Or you may need to make an informed decision about next steps and actions. These reflective moments can be the most difficult in the process.

'The riddle' is a way of reflecting on the course of your research.

It is a set of questions that you can apply after each step and at the level of your project as a whole. We call it the riddle because it helps you to create short narratives or arguments about what you have done and found. You can also use images, graphics and other visual material to do this. It starts with questions and works towards answers. By revisiting and using the riddle regularly, you will build up a collection of findings that are accessible and explainable, and that may lead to conclusions or new research questions. At the same time, you will collect and edit material for sharing and making your research public.

What I asked. The question
I asked while making, reading, observing,
etc. Why I asked this, why this question
sparked my curiosity, and where its
urgency and relevance lies.
> my topic

What I did. The steps I took and
the methods I used to find answers to
my questions, such as experimenting,
mapping sources, talking to experts, etc.
> my actions

What I found. The results of my
actions, such as collected data, recorded
experiences, different perspectives, etc.
> my findings

What I (don't) know.
Reflection on the question, the process, the
findings, etc. What do I know and what is
still unclear? Where to go next?
> my insights

[+] Reflection happens all the time, but if you plan it regularly, it becomes part of a practice.

[+] Circles extend from you to your collaborators, all the way to the environment and the planet.

[+] Articulating what escapes articulation can be done in verbal or visual form, or maybe something else completely.

Why do I do what I do?

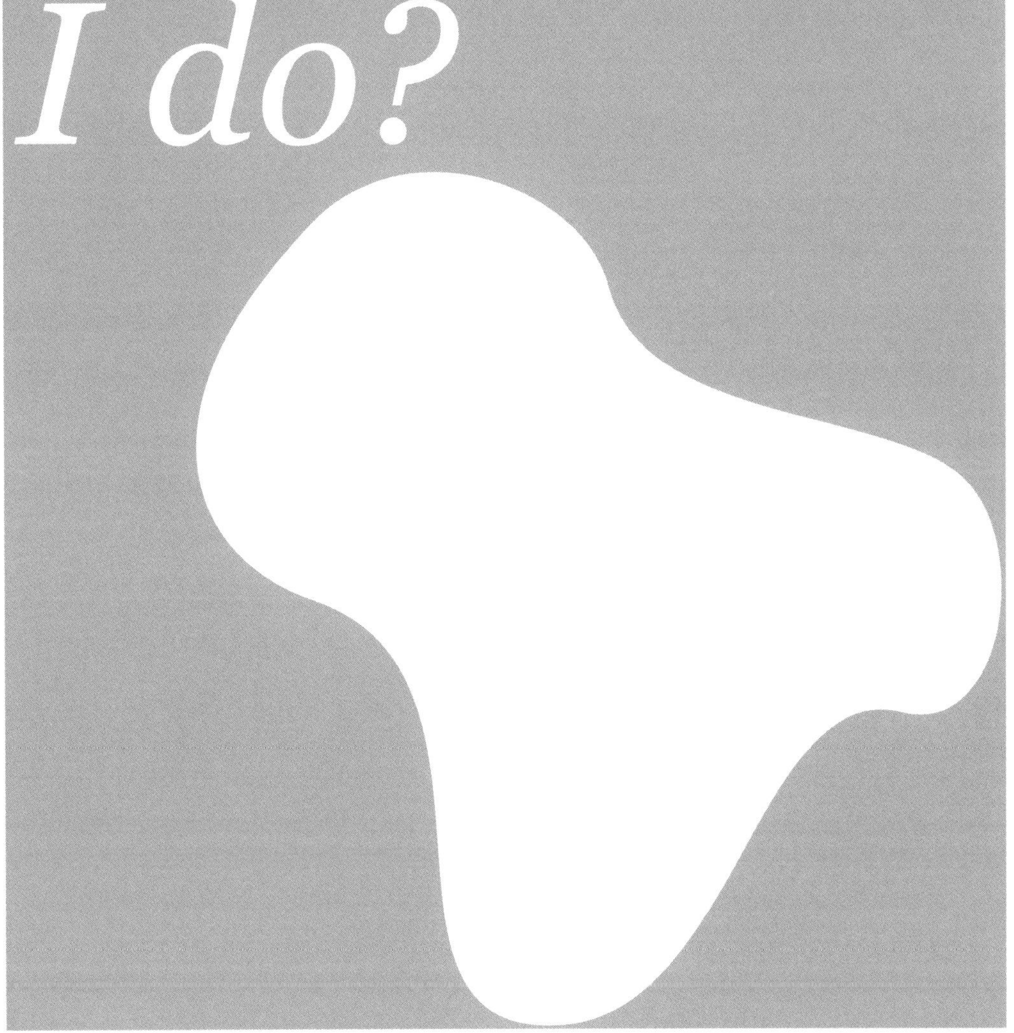

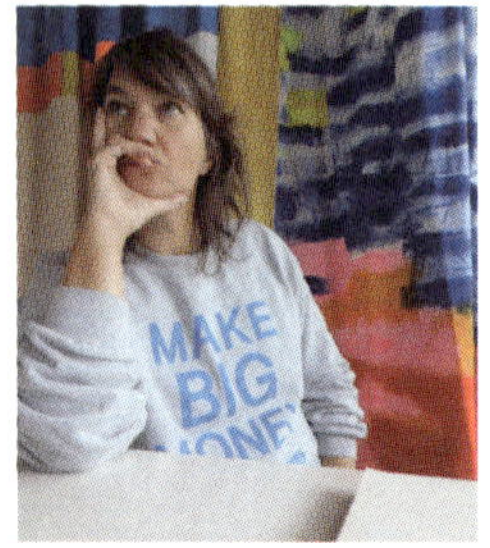

Nanna van Heest is an artist, designer and educator whose interest in colour led her to do design research into the subjective experience people have with colour.

Nanna van Heest | *The Colour Story* | 2020 | Graduation research, MA Master Design, PZI

what if?

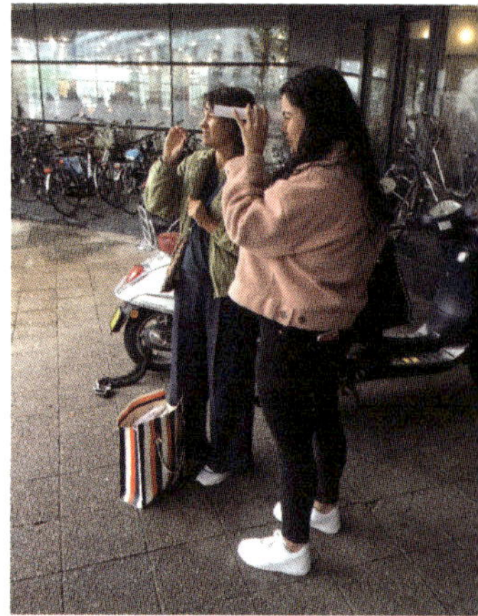

Nanna's experience with and interest in colour clashed with the traditional colour theories of the Bauhaus. Could she gain a deeper understanding of colour and develop a contemporary theory of its ever-changing and elusive properties?

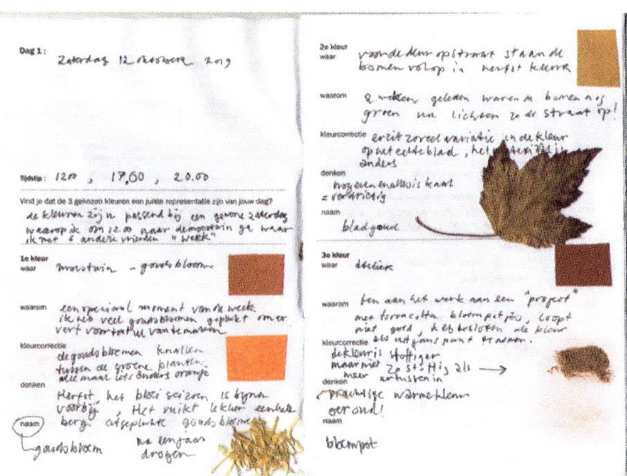

To explore her initial questions, Nanna created a conversation piece. A small canister to look through led to dialogues about what colours stood out for people when they attentively observed the environment. What they saw was very personal and subjective. It facilitated exchange on different connotations and the use of language.

Nanna further explored these subjective responses to colour. She designed material that asked participants to keep a diary of the colour that resonated with them each day. A selection of colour swatches, curated by Nanna, were provided to choose from.

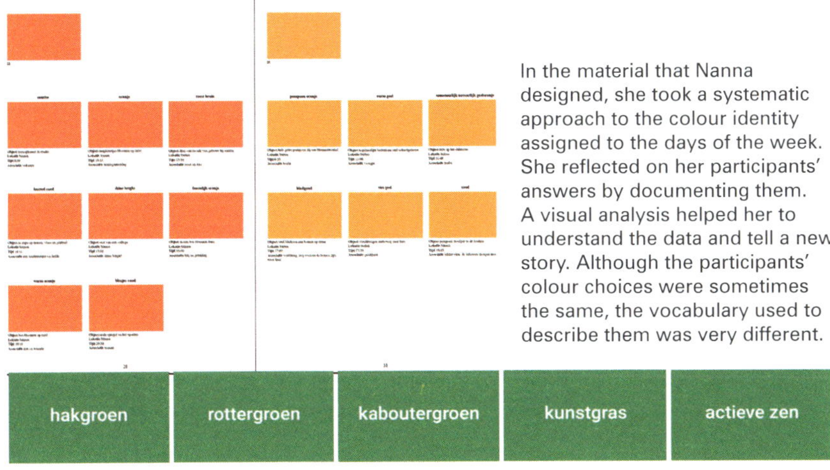

In the material that Nanna designed, she took a systematic approach to the colour identity assigned to the days of the week. She reflected on her participants' answers by documenting them. A visual analysis helped her to understand the data and tell a new story. Although the participants' colour choices were sometimes the same, the vocabulary used to describe them was very different.

Nanna made us of a blog to keep track of material, outcomes and reflections, and to understand and communicate her research. She documented her process in two ways. First, by publishing (visual) results in posts, describing what had been done and how it related to previous actions. Second, she used mapping to draw conclusions and show connections.

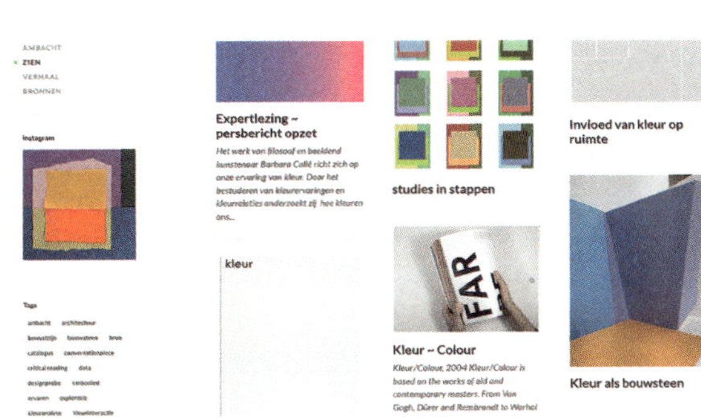

With the method of Emily Noyes Vanderpoel, Nanna contextualised her research into the interaction of colours. This inspired her in different ways of working with notating colour. On the one hand she made graphical analyses of colour and on the other she took notes with a more poetic character.

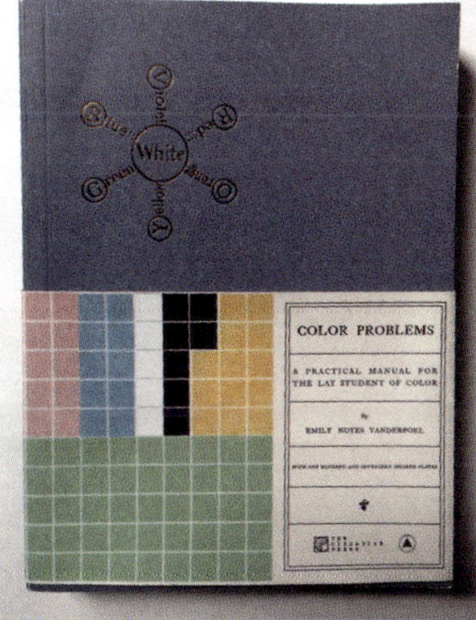

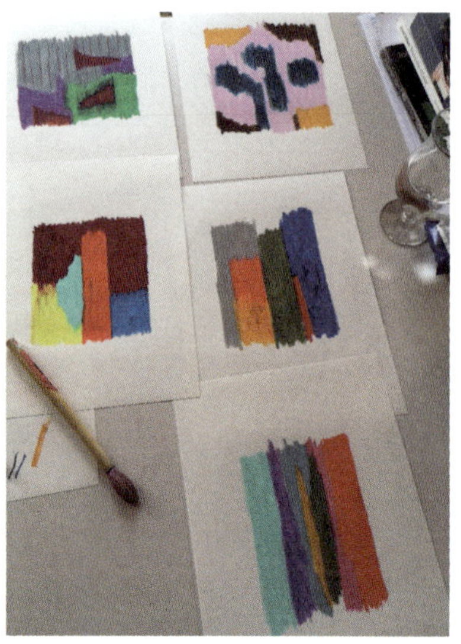

Alongside her search for theoretical context, Nanna was experimenting with colour in order to understand its optical interactions. In a predetermined way, she drew pastel on paper to see how colours combined and what volume each colour needed in relation to the surrounding colours. She made 231 versions during her research and still continues.

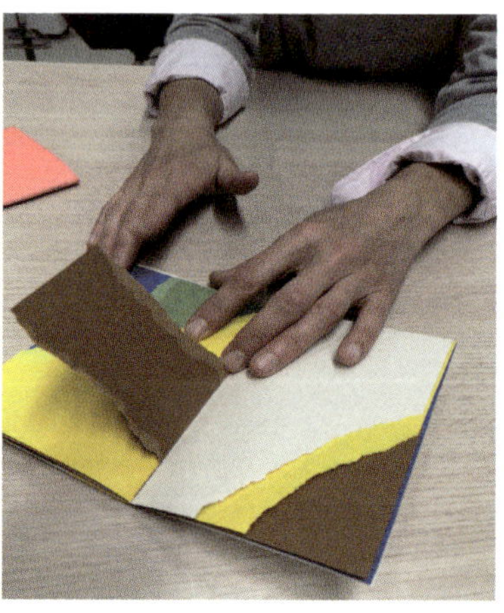

The workshop format also became an important instrument to do participatory research. Nanna's work with participants was influenced by her ongoing experiments. Colour interaction was at the heart of the workshops. In a zine-making workshop she researched how adjacent colours influence each other and how a narrative can be constructed.

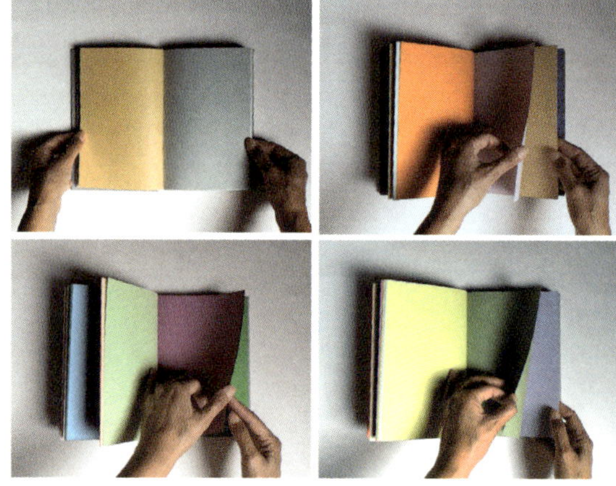

Following up on the zine workshop, Nanna produced a book of coloured paper. The book served as a conversation piece about colour, as well as a way to research its optical effects.

Research

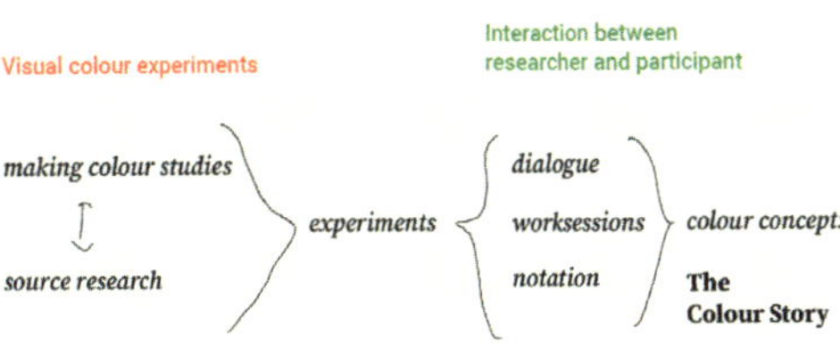

In the last phase of her research, Nanna reflected on all actions in her process by tagging her material and findings with keywords. It helped her to see the relations between participatory research, research of context and research by making.

Nanna's research led to an online publication with two pillars, the online *Cabinet of Curiosities* (*Wonderkamer*) and a thesis. The *Cabinet* is a conceptual free space that gives room to the diverse perspectives on colour as outcomes of her research. The thesis was a way to articulate and communicate the process and the context of the research.

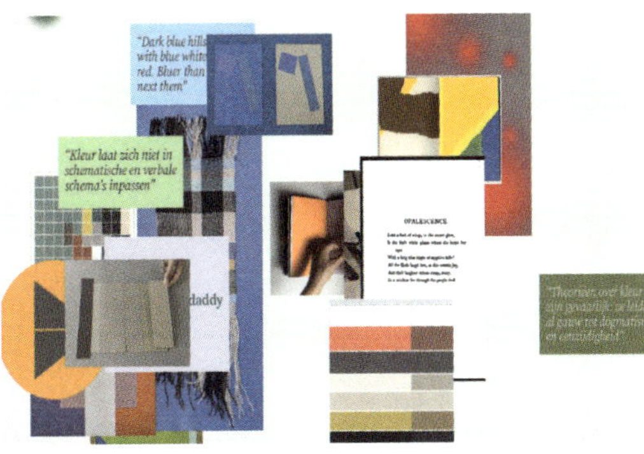

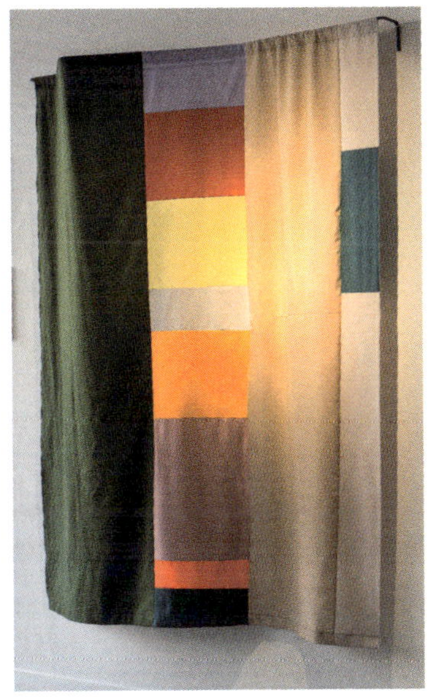

The Colour Story has contributed to a practice where designing workshops and exhibitions, giving lectures and colour advice go hand in hand. Nanna continues her research by exploring a colour literacy program and new ways of colour education as well as an interdisciplinary system of connections between science, art and design, and culture.

#design research
#formulating research questions
#experiental knowledge
#theoretical context
#conversation piece
#dialogues
#designing workshops
#documenting outcomes
#research blog
#processing results
#visual analysis
#contextualising notation systems
#colour notes
#zine making
#online publishing

Where do I leave my traces?

Without documentation, no research. Documenting research findings in a deliberate and transferable way is crucial for analysis and reflection. Start documenting right from the beginning of your project and make sure you do it in an accessible and searchable way, for example by using keywords and categories. Doing so will help you to argue, reflect on and present your research both visually and in writing. Collecting, tagging and structuring different types of information are important actions. They support you in archiving what you have done, deciding what to do next and creating a narrative around your project. In the end, your research documentation may even turn out to be the creative work itself.

For documentation to support your actions and reflections, it is important to pay attention to the structure and system used. Record what you find and where you found it. Findings and insights might first go into a folder called 'research project'. As the project evolves the volume of your documentation will grow and the complexity of your material increases. You will need to apply a system of categorisation, so that you don't lose track of what you've done.

Your documentation can also work for you on a more substantive level if you link it to the content of your research. Add a thematic or topical level to your documentation and return to it regularly. This will also help you to create a meaningful narrative and work towards publication.

Always be critical of what you (don't) document. The archive is a site of power and what is included and excluded can have a huge impact on what is considered knowledge or information, and on who is named and recognised. Try to be inclusive in your documentation practice and reflect on any biases or blind spots that may come through in your use of keywords and tags. You can also take an networked approach by mapping your themes and trying to articulate how they connect, overlap, or remain separate.

How do you link different topics, tags and keywords?

Are the keywords and tags you use specific enough, or perhaps too narrow?

Do the topics that emerge from your documentation cover all aspects of your questions? Do you have any blind spots?

How can your documentation be made meaningful artistically or aesthetically?

begin

When you start a new research project, you often begin by reflecting on previous projects and orientating yourself towards favoured or recurring themes, or open questions.

> Collect ideas, questions, images and other snippets.

> Bring clarity by tagging what is on the (virtual) table and sorting the material into themes.

> Tag the topics and let these tags inform your documentation structure.

> Choose different keywords, colours or even notebooks for each topic.

> Use the keywords to formulate questions and sub-questions, or to guide your analysis, narrative or reflection.

> Don't forget to regularly evaluate the validity of your structure. Are there any missing themes or tags? Which themes aren't used so much?

> Be fastidious about referencing. Include timestamps, URLs and page numbers so that you can easily retrieve sources later.

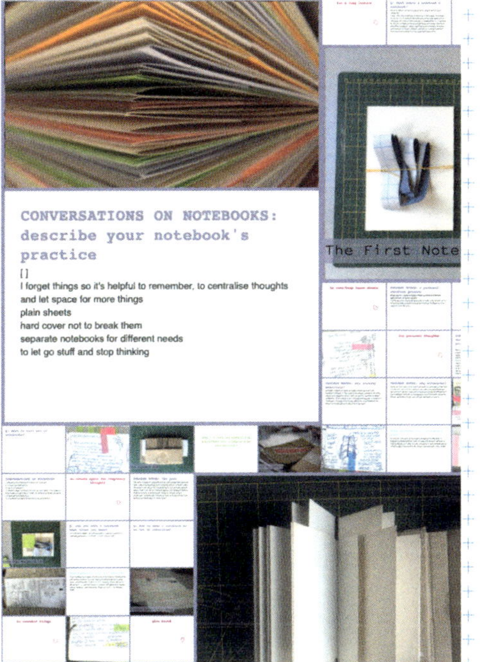

Emma Prato | *How to Make a Notebook That – From Industrial Model to Tool of Expression* | 2023 | Graduation research, MA Experimental Publishing, PZI | The aim of the research was to create a personalised guide to making a notebook that supports individual learning and research needs. A website provides both linear and non-linear ways to do so, next to documenting the research itself.

Repetitie 1
22/2

Warming-up
Eénkoppige worm
Een panty die onze hoofden aan elkaar smolt.
     (Hoofd in elk een heen)
Liggend, kru   l.

Reflectie
* (Kostuum)   **the physical**
* choreograf   Anne asked herself what she saw
het asfalt.   happening between the actors on
                   stage.

De geboorte van de vliegende worm - Anne
[gefilmd]

Een mens, ontwakend, ervaart haar eerste adem. Parallel daaraan
ontwaakt de worm. Langzaam wordt het opgehesen. Terwijl de mens
haar lichaam ontdekt, loopt, om zich heen kijkt. Wordt de worm
de lucht in gehesen.

Reflectie
* Het hijsen van de worm is goed, alleen   **conversations & movement**
context krijgen.
* spel minder doods, de worm wordt niet c   A conversation can be recorded, but
* visdraad, betere worm, misschien meerde   what about observations on body
dynamischer bewegen.   language?
* geluid van de wind buiten werkte heel g

IDEE
* plechtig hijsen, vlaggenmast, kazoo spel.
'Rapapapaaa, nu officieel een vliegende worm!'
Inwijding, doping, ontgroening, ritueel

De geboorte van de vliegende worm - Jonas
[gefilmd]

In het midder   w, net
wormpjes (kar   **temporality**

Hij rent erop   Another challenge was how to   tel
achtig op de   capture meaningful interactions as   in de
buurt.   they unfolded.
Het fysieke s   object.

Dan lukt het, hij heeft het kunnen raken.
Hij draait zijn hoofd naar het publiek en zegt: 'De geboorte
van de vliegende worm - Deel 1'

Gaat met zijn hoofd op de wormen liggen en begint een monoloog.

Monoloog Jonas:
" Ik droomde dat de wind me had uitgewist

M'n silhouet die achterbleef liep door alsof er niks gebeurd

Mug

[Gefilmd]
Maak een scene rond het thema 'Or

Jonas gaat slapen. Mug (Anne) zit
  Net voor hij wegdommelt begint
ergert zich kapot: 'Wat moet dat
Hij probeert het indringende gelu
beestje begint steeds weer als hi
Er ontstaat een kat en muis spel.
zit dat stomme beest? Nergens te
overgeven.

Schrijf oefening

We schreven allemaal een tekst,

Zie 'desk research // schrijfse

Repetitie 3
5/3

                              het bord. Rea
                              eenkomsten, wa

                              de volgende c

'Wie ben ik nog als het stil is'

'Ik besloot te gaan lopen, gewoor

'Had de verkeerde afslag gemaakt,
Het had geregend, dat bracht me

Ik besloot te gaan lopen, gewoor
Anne

Stil. Komt in meditatieve staat,
na lange stilte begint ze haar ha
trekt knopen uit het haar. Loopt
Neemt haar tijd. Tot het haar wee
Gaat weer ze klaar is gaat ze zit
wat ongeduldig bij. Wat aangedaan
Ze heeft gewoon maar iets gedaan.

Ben de weg kwijt
Jonas

[In het steegje tussen het atelie

Fade in -'Sorry, sorry! Mag ik wa

Anne Kloosterboer | *Vliegende Wormen* |
2024 | Graduation research, BA
Transformation Design, WdKA

We begonnen te bewegen, ontdekken en s
later gebruikten we ook onze stem. We
ontstond een gesprek.

Het werkte goed.

het bed.
ug te zoemen. Hij
zijn huis?!'
egeren, maar het
ekker lag.
rechts, links, waar
. Hij zal zich moeten

Kinderspel

Noor zit op een stoel, Jonas era
Ze staat op, de schoenen van Jon
Ze loopt rondjes over het podium
schoenen.

Documentation is often
about keeping track of
sources, recording data
or capturing a process of
experimentation in images.
But what about documenting
the intangible? Art and design
research is often concerned
with that which cannot be
directly seen or measured,
or which has a temporal
or ephemeral quality. For
example, when you work with
people and their emotions
or body movements, or
when you want to capture
a moment from the past or
speculate about the future.
How can you find ways of
documenting what cannot be
straightforwardly recorded
as evidence? Can you find
indirect ways of documenting
that are still articulated and
substantiated?

on-physical

ortant question for her was
document non-physical
ts, like affects and energies in
als.

elt ook met schoenen aa

t, je angst

bij de kapstokken, Jon
kunnen elkaar niet zien, wij hun

miro bord.
rasten, vinden we een

Noor klopt op de muur.
Jonas: 'Hallo!?, ja hallo!'
Noor: Ja hallo!

t 'schrijfsels'

De scene gaat over miscommunicat
spanning in de lucht.

ets te doen'

[De precieze tekst weet ik niet,
opgenomen...]

weg kwijt.
r.'

Repetitie 5
20/3
Noor, Anne

ets te doen

Concept: Hometrainer
Nog niet gemaakt, wel bedacht

...
ammen. Het doet pijn,
end, rondje om de kruk.
en netjes is.
rug op de kruk. Zit er
s er r

Nor fietst op hometrainer richting pub
jecteren we beelden van de stad die fil
de Maastunnel, ff kieke (van heel laag

Je hoort muziek. google maps die zich
t is totale ov

reflections

Anne immediately edited the material
while documenting her observations.

en heerlijk ho
uitgeput. De m
r. Haar hoofd
mgeving doet v
stapelen zich op. Ze raakt uitgeput en
Concept: Alleen in de metro
Nog niet gemaakt, wel bedacht

grote ruimte]

n, sorry' - Fade out

Vliegende Wormen is a montage
theatre performance that uses
improvisation techniques. In
her research project, Anne
investigated the role of the
director, the actors and the space
within improvisational theatre.
She used a notebook to record her
observations and processed these
observations systematically to
formulate new assignments for the
actors.

The importance of images in an art or design research project cannot be overstated. They show or represent what has been made or done, and are used to document the research process. They can be the subject of the art or design research itself, or they can show and clarify what has been studied, found, made or happened. Images help to articulate the research process in a demonstrable way and are vital in making research public.

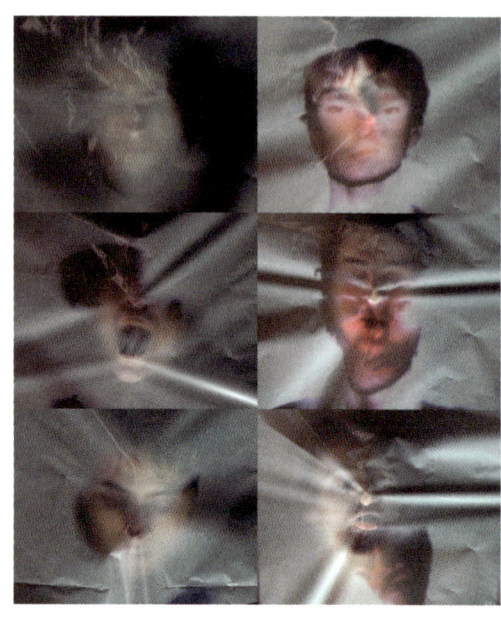

Jilles Pieters | *To Remember Your Dream* | 2024 | Graduation research, BA Audiovisual Design, WdKA | Research into reimagining how 'the screen' can be used in performance art. Iterative experiments with images were important tools for doing research by making and provided the guiding material for the documentation of the research process.

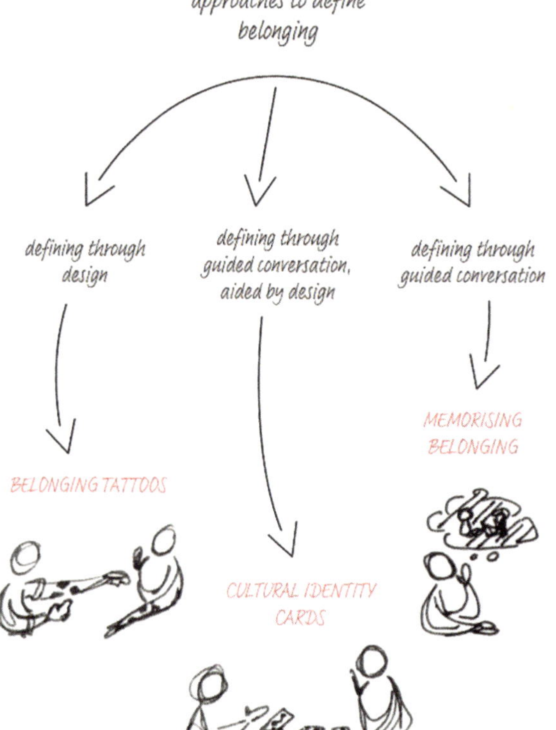

Jet van der Touw | *Defining Belonging* | 2022 | Graduation research, MA Master Design, PZI | A project on how to make discussion about belonging tangible with design research methods. Visualisations of the use of and relationship between methods, roles and designed material clarify how Jet worked with participants at different stages of her research.

> showing 'what is'

Images that record what is happening at a given moment. Living beings or tangible things are observed and captured in (audio)visual form.
Observations of: a meeting, home, street, work, a person, people, animals, buildings, nature, etc.

> showing creative work

Images that represent or show your creative work and research, or that of others. As part of the documentation process, collections of images need to be categorised thematically and, for example, time-stamped.
Representations of: material experiments, artworks, designs, collections, art historical-, self made- and found images, etc.

> showing processes

Images that present more or less complex information and insights from your research. This is done using the visual language of maps, timelines, diagrams, storyboards, etc.
Designs of: methods, workflows, interactions, networks, systems, results, geographical, scientific or historical facts, etc.

How do you make the invisible visible?

How do you show the process of making?

What is the role of visual metaphor in your research?

How can you assemble a series of images to make your research public?

Each action in doing research involves documentation. The actions from the 'base' of the circle model – research by making, research of context, participatory research – will produce outcomes such as information, images, prototypes, encounters and experiences. Documentating these outcomes always involves reflection. Through the act of documenting, you process the results and analyse their meaning. Documenting data and outcomes is also an important step towards meaningful representation. The process of reflection, selection and editing leads toward making your research public.

Choosing the best means and most appropriate media for documenting your research activities and findings can be challenging. Remember that these means and media can be as diverse as the questions you ask and the actions you take. A well-considered choice of means and media can support both your process and your content. Ultimately, they will guide you towards the moment of making public. Ask yourself which means and media you are comfortable with, or want to explore.

DOCUMENTING RESEARCH

archive
automate
capture
code
collect
draw
film
listen
observe
photograph
record
scrape
sketch
survey
take notes
vlog

REFLECTING ON RESEARCH

analyse
argue
ask
assess
categorise
compose
connect
edit
evaluate
iterate
paraphrase
position
question
quote
select
tag
transcribe
value

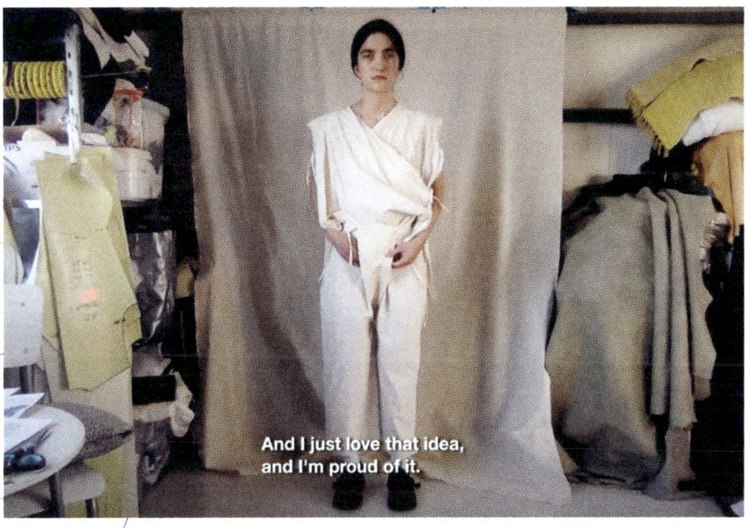

Linn Alleman | *The Closer One Looks, the More Clear it Becomes* | 2020 | Graduation research, BA Fashion Design, WdKA | A research project around the question of how to give folkloric clothing a modern touch and express your heritage at the same time. An important part of her research were Linn herself and how clothes are an extension of her identity. She fitted all the prototypes of her collection herself and captured this by photographing the experiments. Linn recorded her more conceptual thought processes in weekly video reports.

MAKING
PUBLIC

blog
cite
discuss
exhibit
inform
interact
organise
publish
reference
show
tell
typeset
upload
write

- [+] *A documentation structure will help you keep track of your research and help your thinking.*

- [+] *Things go by before you know it – capture them while you can.*

- [+] *Attention to documentation helps in making public – documentation can even become a work of art in itself.*

- [ ]

- [ ]

- [ ]

Where do I leave my traces?

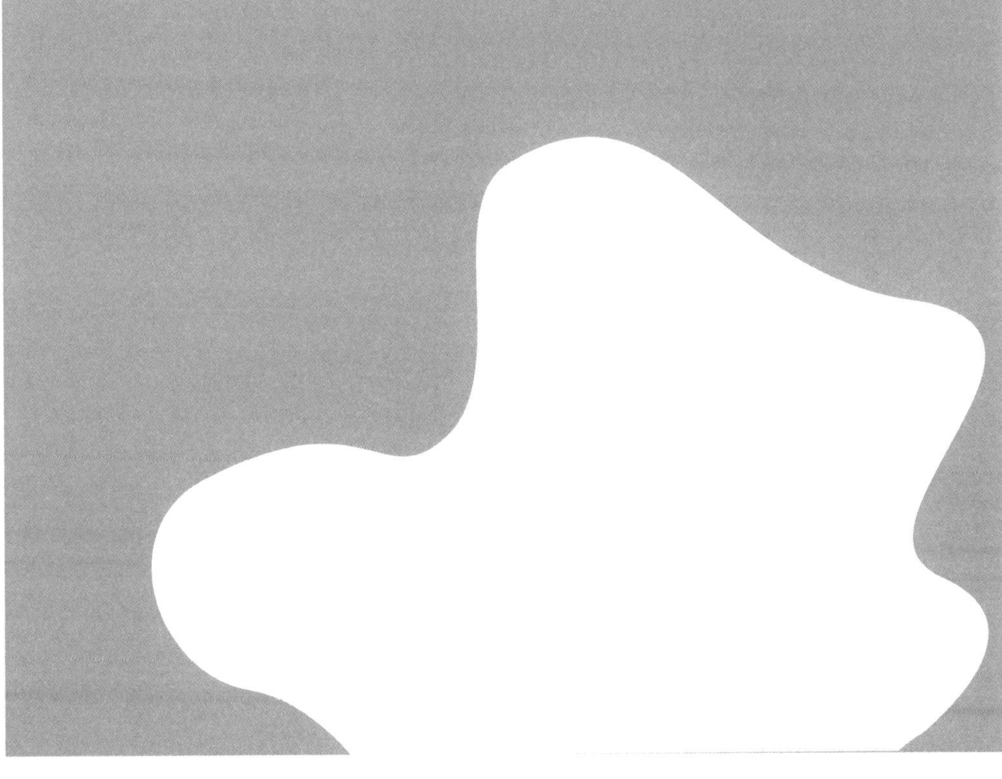

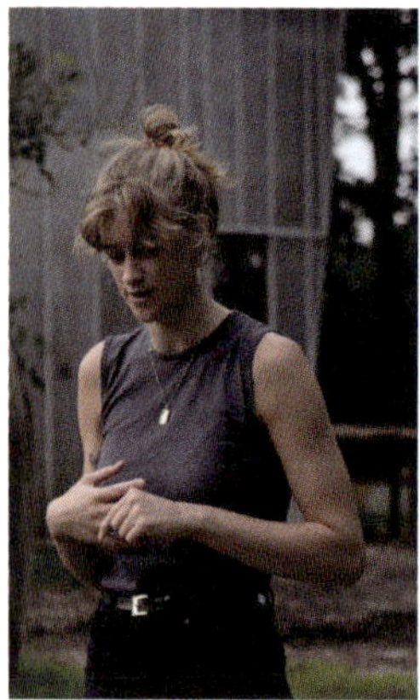

Cid Pijnenburg graduated in 2024 as a transformation designer. For her research, she wanted to find out how young people could better understand themselves through touch.

Cid Pijnenburg | *Touchscape* | 2024 | Graduation research BA, Transformation Design, WdKA

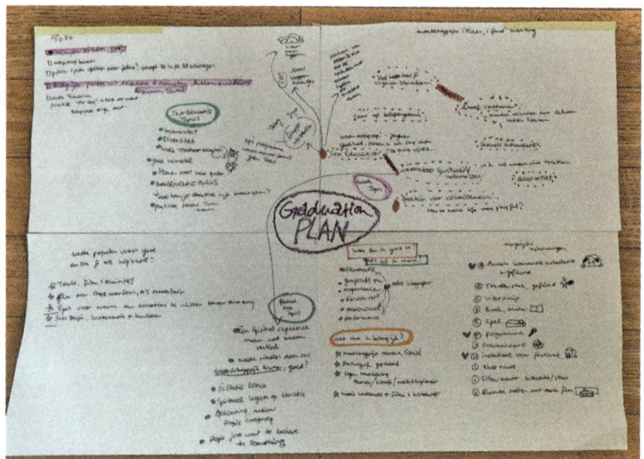

Already prior to her studies, Cid had the idea of travelling to different schools in a van with sensory objects. During her studies she used her projects to explore feminism. When sex education in schools came under pressure in the Netherlands as a result of the political shift to the right, the idea for her graduation research took shape. To concretise her ideas, she made a mind map. In this map she linked everything she found interesting and had researched in previous projects.

For Cid it was important to make, think and contextualise at the same time. She started experimenting with touching objects. Based on the idea that one holds one's mobile phone more than one's lover, she filmed herself touching her mobile phone. This was the beginning of a series of short videos in which she touched different objects.

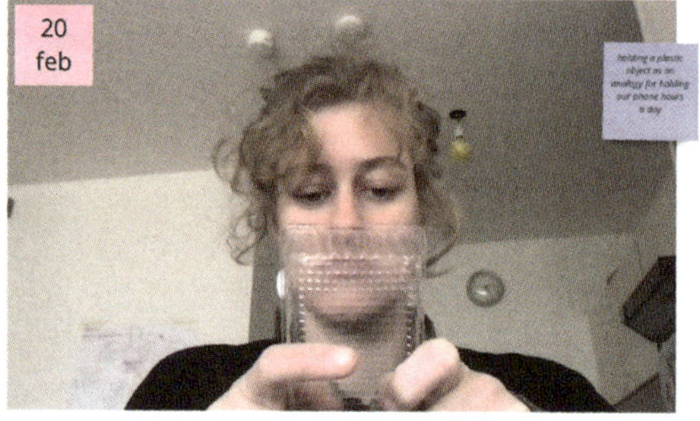

To find a language for what she was working on, Cid looked to artists and designers with similar making practices. In Melanie Bonajo's work, for example, she found meaningful terms, and in Bruno Munari's 'tactile workshops' she recognised a common language. Studying the work of others confirmed for her that she could continue along the path she had chosen. She documented and classified all the found material and her reflections on an online Miroboard.

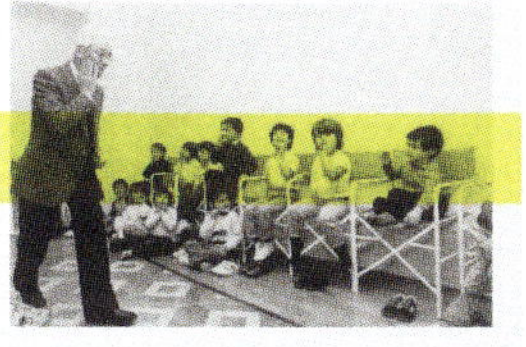

DO NO TOUCH! How many times do children hear this order? No one would ever say: do not look, do not listen, but touching is different. Evidently a lot of people think you can do without. *The tactile workshops* is one of the books from the **Workshop series** that describes different working, techniques, from educational to explanatory pamphlets and "poetic" play… With basic explanations and plenty of stimuli, suggestions and maps to get adults and children, teachers and students working together.

DO NOT TOUCH

With the question in mind of what we touch each day, Cid went in search in her own home of things that she herself touches in one day. She collected and documented these objects. The compilation grew into an library of objects called *Object I like to touch and interact with Library*.

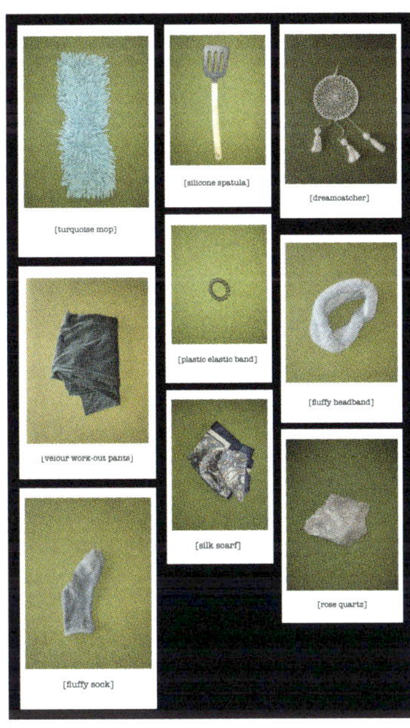

In order to broaden her research, Cid asked other people to choose objects from the library and tell her what they felt when they touched them. The tests demonstrated that the objects needed to be more abstract, as the meaning or purpose of the objects was getting in the way of the sensation. With two product designer friends Cid designed new objects. The shapes were made by hand using modelling clay and then 3D printed to make them more manageable and durable.

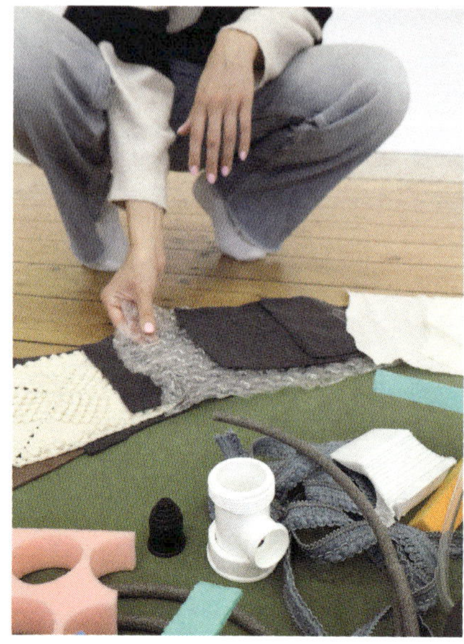

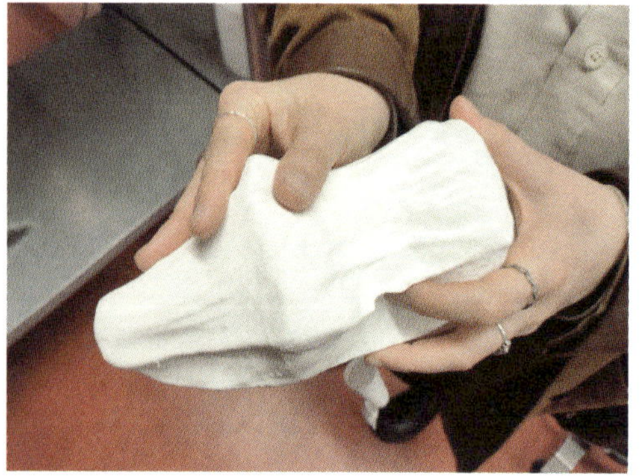

In dialogue with one of her graduation supervisors, Cid had the idea to divide her library of objects into two: a collection of existing objects and a series of new forms.

The purpose of the project was becoming clear to Cid: she wanted young adults to become aware of touch and how it can help them to reflect on who they are, what their desires are and what their boundaries are. As this is a sensitive subject, Cid met with experts in the field, a sexologist and a drama therapist.

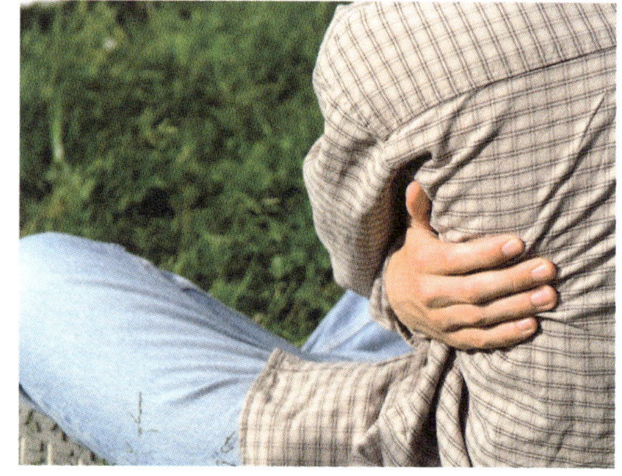

Cid designed a workshop using the advice of the experts. Alongside her objects, she incorporated safety measures and experiences from mindfulness workshops. She wrote a script for guiding the workshop.

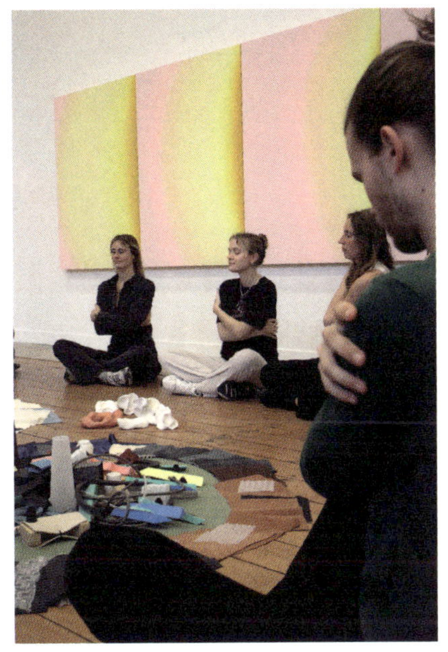

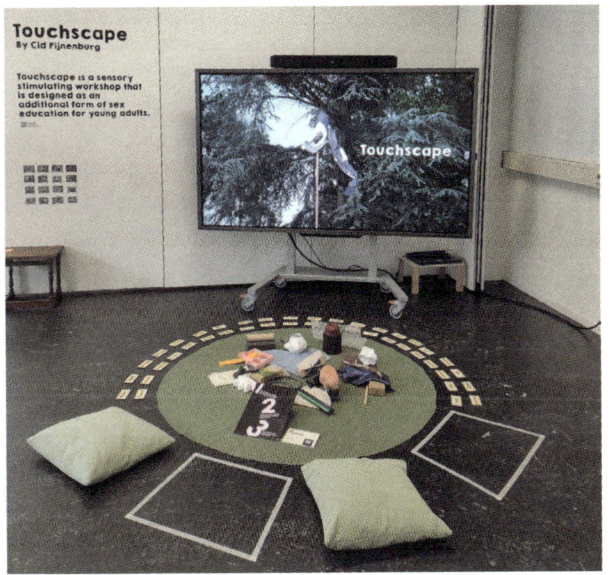

Cid's final graduation project consisted of the two collections of objects, a guide with the script to help young adults use the objects and two different recordings of the workshop on film.

#mapping inspiration
#reflecting on themes
#talking to experts
#tactile research
#recording outcomes
#finding vocabulary
#researching other artists
  and designers
#collecting objects
#selecting objects
#testing objects
#taking pictures
#designing new objects
#curating objects
#working with participants
#designing a workshop
#testing a workshop
#editing videos
#making a script
#designing a final
  presentation

What is research without a public?

Making public is part and parcel of doing research.

Of course, you can always delve into your own curiosity, ask questions that primarily concern yourself, or decide that your findings or results are not suitable for sharing with others. But a research project that is confined to your own computer or studio misses an important dimension. It is only by bringing your research into contact with the outside world that you can fully appreciate its validity and reach. Art and design research, in particular, is thoroughly connected to the public. It is good practice to share the research that has gone into the creative work with the public.

Your research is finished, you've drawn conclusions,

made a work or written up your findings in a research document, and now it's time to share it with others. But the act of making public is not just the end point, as is often thought. Here we propose that making public is part of the research itself – whether it is in the form of a workshop, an exhibition or the pre-publication of a paper. Organising a public moment can help you in your process, for example when you get stuck or feel the need to refine your questions. Working towards a moment of making public will force you to think about the broader context and take on an outsider's perspective, which can be very fruitful. Again, particularly in art and design, where the public is such an important part of the context, there are plenty of good reasons to treat making public as an integral part of the iterative process of your research.

Who is a possible audience for your work? Can you think of other groups you could reach?

What do you want the public to get out of your work? What would you like to get from the public?

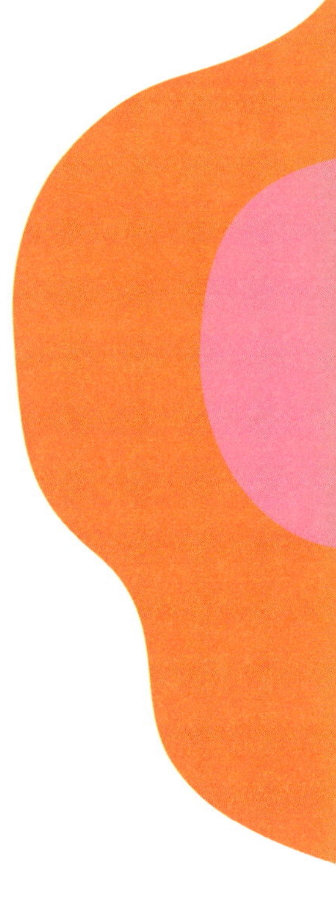

try out

How will you document the responses, comments and experiences that come up?

How can you translate them into the next step?

> Hold a workshop where you can present your methodology and let others work with it.

> Publish a series of blog posts about your sources and any questions you may have.

> Set up a small exhibition and talk to visitors.

> Give a presentation of your work-in-progress to your peers and leave plenty of time for discussion.

> Translate the feedback in a next iterative step.

Making public before the research is complete allows you to:
> *get feedback on your sources, results, design, presentation and storytelling;*
> *offer preliminary findings to your intended audience or your peers;*
> *engage and share with others reciprocally;*
> *begin to build a public or community around your research topic or practice.*

The making public of your **research** doesn't have to be limited to one type of audience. Nor does it have to be limited to publishing words on paper or on screen. Thinking about who you want to reach, what you want them to take away from your research and what formats are appropriate can lead to a hybrid publishing strategy. You talk differently to a potential buyer of your work than you do to your peers. Likewise, you probably engage differently with your childhood friends, the stranger scrolling through your socials and the avid reader downloading an essay from your website.

Who would you like to be your public?

Who do you think will be your public?

art buyers
cinema-goers
classmates
collaborators
colleagues
collectors
family members
friends
gallery owners
influencers
journalists
museum visitors
neighbours
participants
peers
readers
respondents
scholars
school children
tutors
web surfers
YouTube viewers

Consider the accessibility of your work when mapping your publics and choosing appropriate media. This can be in terms of content, format and physical space. For example, text can be easy to understand (even for non-native speakers) or dense and jargon-laden. A long academic paper can be adapted to a blog post or even summarised in bullet points. When it comes to format, be aware of certain exclusions that a medium may bring with it. A podcast will not be accessible to someone with a hearing impairment, but that can be addressed by adding a transcript. A website full of options or moving elements may be fun, but can be a barrier for users with low bandwidth internet or who are neurodiverse. Finally, if you are using a space for a workshop or meeting, check its accessibility and communicate this clearly.

The afterlife of publication

is another factor to take into account. Making public can take place during the research and the results can be shared once the research is complete. It can be worth thinking about what happens to your work in the longer term. All too often, and understandably, attention tends to fade after a while. What kind of afterlife do you want for your publication? Where will it be archived? How will you make sure that someone who's interested can still find it?

branch out

> Map different publics. They can be general and specific, insiders and outsiders, likely, unlikely, sought after or stumbled upon, now and in the future.

> Decide on the focus for each of the publics. Who knows what? How much do you need to explain? What do you want them to remember? What action do you want them to take?

> Consider different media and formats. Written publications, visual or non-verbal publications, 'live' media and everything in between.

> Link the different media to different publics. They can be online and offline, free and paid for, with high involvement or low threshold. Also consider accessibility.

While making your research
public can take many shapes
and forms, especially in art and design,
publishing and writing are likely to be
involved in one way or another.
Publishing formats can range from the
traditional book or article to more visual
forms such as graphics, film essays or even
comics and graffiti, and thus are not limited
to textual or verbal forms. But whether you
are working on a vlog, an animation or an
exhibition, chances are you will be doing
some writing along the way.

Writing can be daunting, especially for
those who are visually oriented. But it doesn't
have to be. Writing can be an experimental
and artistic practice like any other. Treat
language as a material that you can try
out and play with, and learn to use more
effectively.

One way to approach writing and
publishing in an experimental way is to think
about the relationship between form and
content. If you are researching diaries, why
not write in diary form? If you're researching
social media, why not use social media as
your format? You can write on fabric, in yarn,
with paint or flowers, on the wall or in the
street.

You don't have to choose one format and
leave the other. Hybridity means that you
mix and match different formats – online and
offline – according to your needs and the
needs of your public. In addition, each of the
different publics identified may demand its
own approach or format. With some effort,
you can multiply your audience and learn
more about what matters most to them and
to you.

album
atlas
billboard
cartography
clothing emblem
code
comic
data visualisation
exhibition
film essay
get-together
graphic novel
Instagram story
installation
interview
lecture
non-linear narrative
online map
open-access article
performance
presentation
reading club
screening
short story
song
TikTok video
visual essay
vlog
workshop
zine

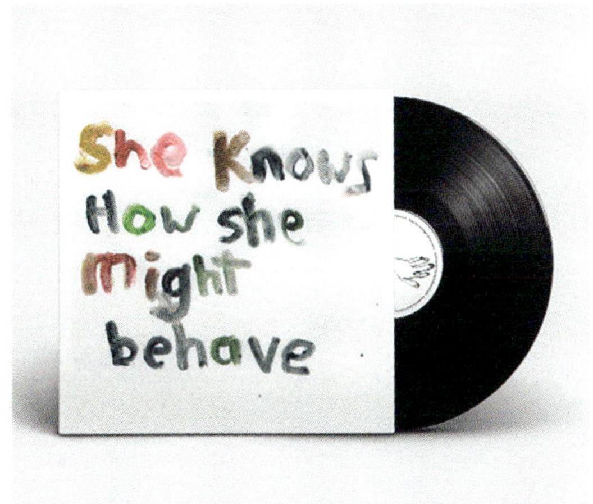

Tracy Hanna | *She Knows How She Might Behave* | 2016 | MA Fine Art, PZI | Research published in the format of a 7" EP. The publication also contains a twenty page booklet with the lyrics to 'songs', two of which can be listened to on the record.

Nienke Galjaard | *Ghar* | 2018 | BA Product Design, WdKA | A bar of soap turned into a medium for publishing. Texts from the research on Syrian refugees are pressed into a bar of Aleppo soap. When used, the texts will fade away.

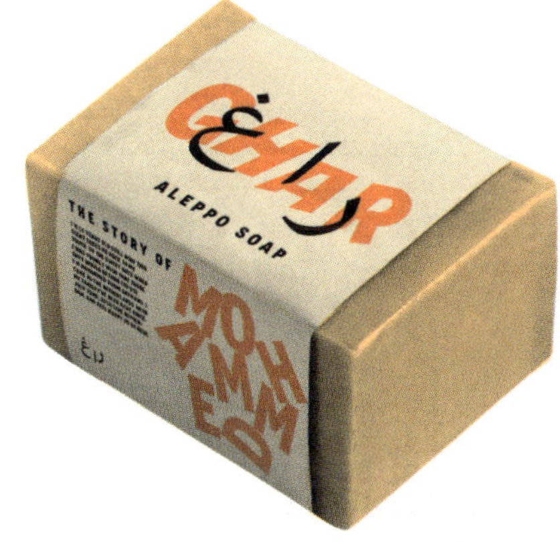

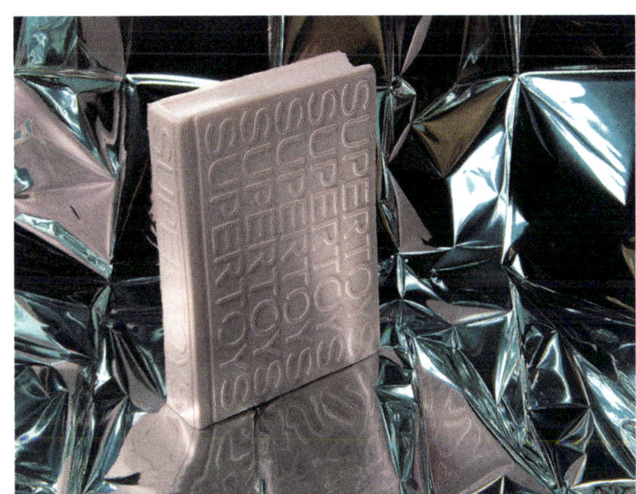

Merle Flügge | *Supertoys Supertoys: Objects of the Imaginary* | 2017 | MA Master Interior Architecture: Research + Design, PZI | A publication in different formats including a sponge shaped like a book and an electronic publication.

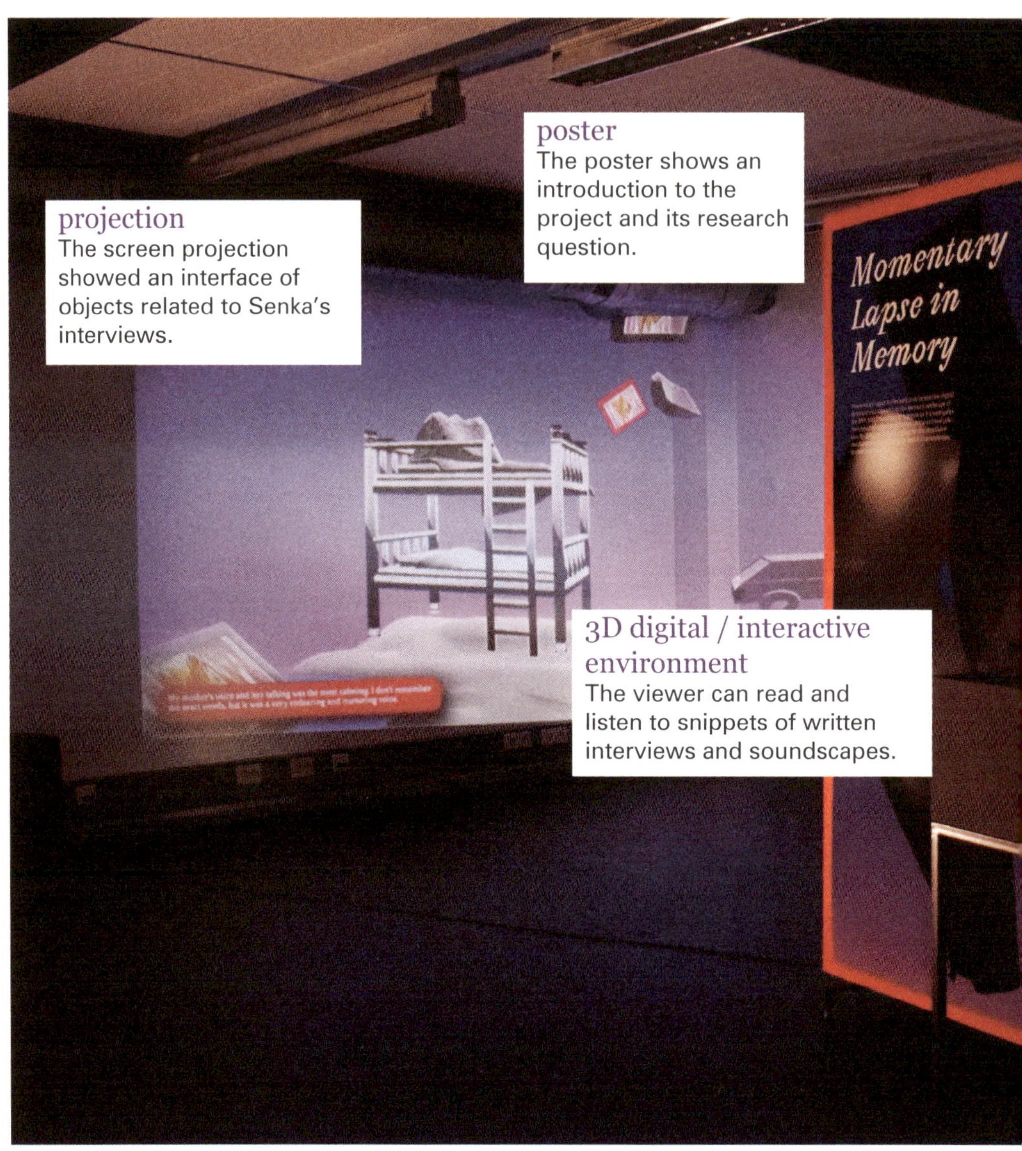

Senka Milutinović | *Momentary Lapse in Memory* | 2020 | Graduation research, BA Graphic Design, WdKA

printed leporello

A reflective writtten publication on the process of making and the methods used.

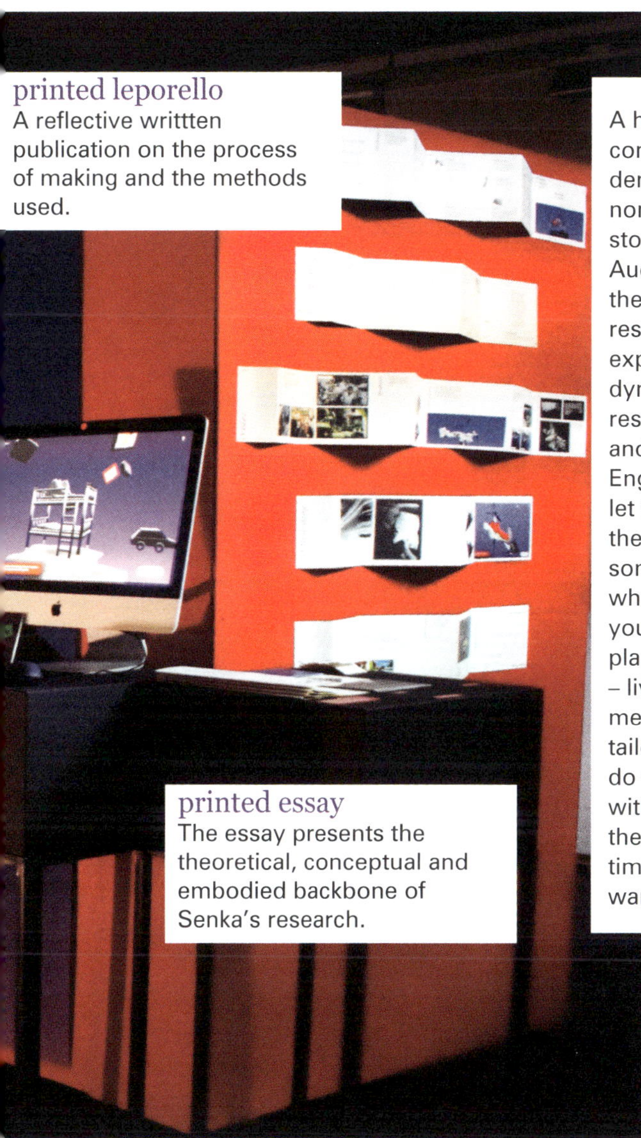

printed essay

The essay presents the theoretical, conceptual and embodied backbone of Senka's research.

A hybrid installation or constellation of elements can demonstrate the multifaceted, non-linear and complex stories of your research. Audiences engage with the work in different ways, resulting in a rich and varied experience. Let them move dynamically through the research process, pausing and moving on as they see fit. Engage them in conversation, let them interact with the work and give them something to take with them when they leave. Or find your audience in different places and at different times – live, on paper or on social media, with stories and media tailored to the occasion. What do you want them to take with them? What do you want them to remember in a year's time? Is there anything you want them to do?

Momentary Lapse in Memory is an interactive digital environment concerning the memory landscape of the 1999 NATO bombing of Yugoslavia. It questions the creation of monumental narratives that weaponise collective memory and inquires how oral histories of traumatic events can exist without being instrumentalised. In doing so, it creates space for the unreliable mechanisms of memory and its transmission, for it to steer and sway.

- [+] *Making public does not have to be the end of a project, it might be a new beginning.*

- [+] *Consider the relation between medium and message and public.*

- [+] *Sharing is caring.*

What is research without a public?

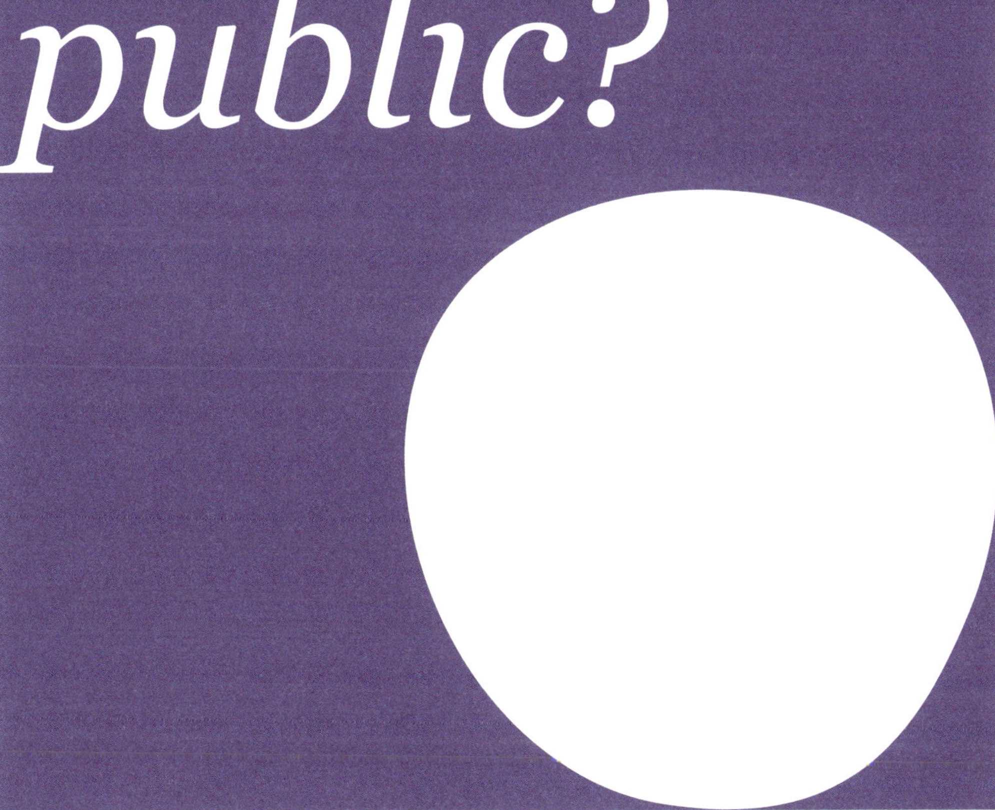

Below you find a list of articles, books and websites for further reference. It is limited to easily accessible or classic works and to the most used sources for this book.

Hands On Research for Artists, Designers & Educators was conceived as a kind of prequel to *Research for People Who (Think They) Would Rather Create* by Dirk Vis (Onomatopee, 2021). Where that book deals mostly with the research document, this guide starts from the very beginning of a research project.

RESEARCH BY MAKING

Methods for experimenting with materials, designs and making in general: Annemiek van Boeijen, Jaap Daalhuizen and Jelle Zijlstra, *Delft Design Guide: Perspectives – Models – Approaches – Methods*, BIS publishers, 2020.

Strategies for making: Emiel Heijnen and Melissa Bremmer, *Wicked Art Assignments*, Valiz, 2020.

On iteration and possible research cycles: *Design Thinking Bootleg*, d.school at Stanford University, 2010, https://dschool. stanford.edu/resources/design-thinking-bootleg.

RESEARCH OF CONTEXT

Extensive database for referencing, evaluating sources and citation: *Purdue Online Writing Lab*, https://owl.purdue.edu/owl/index.html.

Using the library as a resource and a medium: Heide Hinrichs, Elizabeth Haines and Jo-ey Tang, *Shelf Documents: Art Library as Practice*, Royal Academy of Fine Arts Antwerp, 2020.

Handbook and guide for diversity in research of context: Linda Tuhiwai Smith, *Decolonizing Methodologies: Research and Indigenous Peoples*, Bloomsbury, 2023.

Ongoing search for sources as an artistic project: Ryan Gander, 'Loose Associations and Other Lectures', https://inputparty.nl/wp-content/uploads/2019/02/gander-ryan-loose-associations.pdf.

PARTICIPATORY RESEARCH

Ins and outs of participatory research in the arts and design field: Liesbeth Huybrechts (ed.), *Participation Is Risky: Approaches to Joint Creative Processes*, Valiz, 2014.

A book exploring how collective action can take shape in art and design: Janneke Wesseling and Florian Cramer, *Making Matters: A Vocabulary for Collective Arts*, Valiz, 2022.

Toolkit for setting up collaborative projects which includes everything you need to think and talk about: *Toolkit for Cooperative, Collective, & Collaborative Cultural Work*, Press Press & The Institute for Expanded Research, 2020.

Toolkit for transformative learning and research: Kelli Rose Pearson, Malin Bäckman, Sara Grenni, Angela Moriggi, Siri Pisters and Anke de Vrieze, *Arts-Based Methods for Transformative Engagement*, SUSPLACE, 2018.

REFLECTING ON RESEARCH

The role of questions in arts and design research: James Haywood Rolling Jr., 'Artistic Method in Research as a Flexible Architecture for Theory-Building', *International Review of Qualitative Research*, Vol. 7, No. 2, Summer 2014, pp. 161-168.

On ethical questions in the arts and design: Jostein Gundersen, Nina Malterud, Aslaug Nyrnes, Anne-Helen Mydland, Hans Knut Sveen, 'Map ethics! A method for identifying and addressing ethical dimensions of artistic research projects', *Research Catalogue*, 2022, https://www.researchcatalogue.net/view/699306/1167400?c=1.

How different artists deal with ethical issues in their work: Walead Beshty (ed.), *Ethics*, Documents of Contemporary Art, Whitechapel Gallery and the MIT Press, 2015.

DOCUMENTING RESEARCH

An online platform for documenting
and making public artistic research:
The Research Catalogue, https://www.
researchcatalogue.net/portal/about.

The role of the image in research and
its documentation: Nikolaus Gansterer,
Drawing a Hypothesis: Figures of Thought,
Springer, 2011.

Practical guide on how to keep a research
journal and how to make the most of it:
Nicole Brown, *Making the Most of Your
Research Journal*. Policy Press, 2021.

MAKING PUBLIC

The Hybrid Publishing Research Award
series (Willem de Kooning Academy, 2016-
2021) is showcased on pp. 90-91.

Practice-based research into hybrid
publishing strategies for art publications:
*Here and Now? Explorations in Urgent
Publishing*, Institute of Network Cultures,
2020.

Interviews with many artists about their
research practice: Lucy Cotter (ed.),
Reclaiming Artistic Research, Hatje Cantz,
2024.

The Circle of Doing Research model that this book is structured around was developed at the Willem de Kooning Academy (WdKA) and the Piet Zwart Institute (PZI) with the intention of creating a shared research vocabulary for students and tutors, available to all disciplines and all levels from first year to masters. Through conversations with numerous colleagues and students, it grew into a model for understanding and teaching research specifically geared to a practice-based environment. Without these conversations, this book would not have become a reality. It is truly a collaborative effort, informed by countless encounters, dialogues and exchanges with others. We are grateful to all the colleagues and students at WdKA and PZI for their insights, suggestions and enthusiasm over the past three years as we have developed and worked with this model. We hope that this book will bring energy and insight to others as it has to us.

Title: Hands on Research for Artists, Designers & Educators

Set Margins #35

Authors: Miriam Rasch, Harma Staal, Jojanneke Gijsen

Design: Harma Staal

Copyeditor: Clementine Edwards

Contributors: Aldje van Meer, Cleo Foole, Deanna Herst, Hanneke Briër, reinaart vanhoe, Wilma Knol

Proofreaders: Anne Weijers, Florian Cramer, Herman Duchenne, Leah Howd, Kimmy Spreeuwenberg, Renée Spanjer

Images: we have made every effort to clear all rights for image reproductions and to identify all the owners of copyright. In case of doubt, contact us at wdka.researchstation@hr.nl
© Images by the artists/designers, except if stated otherwise here. Houses (10) by Runs Codol Gonzales | Rink Schelling trajectory: portrait (16) and making work (18) by Ilse Oudheusden, samples (18) by Wesley van Zutphen | Victoria McGuire trajectory: portrait (32), models and exhibition (35) by Tim Sluijter, man in suit (32) by Paola Puntar | Nanna van Heest trajectory: watch tube (32) by Karla de Witte, textile (35) by Marlies Lageweg | Shanti Versnel, photo by Annick Santen (40) | Esther Verhamme, game ©Ficklefish (43) | Cid Pijnenburg trajectory: hand (82) by Sanne Kaal, workshop (83) by Joop Pijnenburg

Publisher: Set Margins'

Printer: UAB Petro ofsetas, Vilnius, LT

ISBN: 9789083404165

Published in collaboration with the Research Center Willem de Kooning Academy, Rotterdam University of Applied Sciences

First print November 2024, 4.500 copies
Second print April 2025, 3.500 copies
Third print January 2026, 4.000 copies